D1001932

Searching

for

Isabel

Godin

 EARCHING

FOR

 SABEL

 ODIN

CELIA WAKEFIELD

CHICAGO
REVIEW
PRESS

Library of Congress Cataloging-in-Publication Data

Wakefield, Celia
    Searching for Isabel Godin / Celia Wakefield.
        p.   cm.
    Includes index.
    ISBN 1-55652-225-8
    1. Godin des Odonais, Isabelle de Grandmaison, b. 1728?—
Journeys—Amazon River Region. 2. Amazon River Region—
Description and travel. 3. Godin des Odonais, Jean, 1712–
1792. 4. Mission géodésique (France) 5. Ecuador—
Biography. 6. France—Biography. I. Title.
F2546.W17   1994
918.1104′3—dc20   94-21527
                                                                          CIP

Details from photographs courtesy of Bancroft Library.
Maps by Gerald Charm.

Published by Chicago Review Press, Incorporated
814 North Franklin Street, Chicago, Illinois, 60610

Printed in the United States of America

ISBN: 1–55652–225–8

1   2   3   4   5   6   7   8   9   10

To the members of
AMITIE BERRY-CHIMBORAZO
who keep alive the memory of
Isabel Godin and the French Mission

ACKNOWLEDGMENTS

MANY PEOPLE IN VARIOUS countries have helped me with advice, encouragement, and information. I could not have written this book without them.

In France: Mark and Sylviane Lemaire, Marcel and Germaine Robin, Bernard Vannier.

In Mexico: Beryl Buchanan, Naomi Boulton, Barbara Covarrubias, Dorothy Howland, Marne Martin, Sharon Orozco, Robert Somerlott.

In the United States: Diane Capito, Gerry Charm, Elizabeth LeCount, Marian Rust-Charm, Larry and Betty Waldron.

**Expedition Route
France to Quito**

Caribbean Sea

Santo Domingo

FROM
FRANCE

Martinique

Portobelo
Panama

Cartagena

QUITO

Manta

Guayaquil

─────────── Route of Expedition
·················· La Condamine & Bouquer, Manta to Quito
─ ─ ─ ─ ─ ─ Other Expedition Members, Guayaquil to Quito

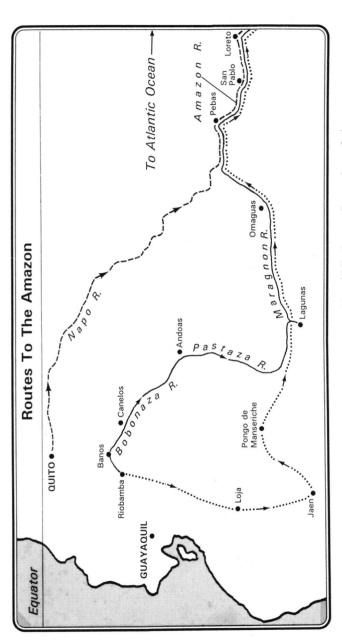

Routes To The Amazon

Equator

QUITO

To Atlantic Ocean

Napo R.

GUAYAQUIL

Riobamba

Banos

Canelos

Bobonaza R.

Andoas

Pastaza R.

Loja

Pongo de Manseriche

Jaen

Lagunas

Maragnon R.

Omaguas

Amazon R.

Pebas

San Pablo

Loreto

---- Usual Missionary Route from Quito

——— Route taken by Maldonado, Jean Godin, Isabel Godin

·········· River Route taken by La Condamine

ONE

Ecuador, November 1989

"THE EQUATOR," CRIED ANTONIO, my taxi driver, grinning. "The tropics, Señorita, the tropics!" He stamped his feet for warmth.

I pulled my sweater around my shoulders. The day was chilly. At an altitude of nine thousand feet it had a right to be, even here at the equator, the mitad del mundo. We had driven a few miles from Quito and stood now on a bare plain surrounded by sheer snowy peaks. The imaginary equatorial line lay at my feet. I looked along a short paved avenue to the monument. It stood foursquare, ugly, no frills, marked on the sides with big letters, *N*, *E*, *S*, and *W*. An elevator within the monument allowed the visitor—there weren't many yet this morning—to mount to an observation post for the viewing of white volcanoes and a sapphire sky where feathery clouds drifted. Down on the avenue a tour group loitered, snapping each others' pictures as they straddled one foot north, one south of the line.

I took a few photos of the monument, then noticed some statues on pedestals bordering the avenue.

"What are those?" I asked Antonio.

"Those were members of the French Expedition"—he waved a hand in dismissal—"a long time ago, Señorita."

I inspected them. The sculptor must have admired things Roman, for each of the busts showed an almost identical heavyset man of middle age, solemn, with aquiline features, the perfect model of a centurion. They wore elaborate wigs and stared disapprovingly into space. I read the inscriptions: *Charles-Marie de La Condamine, Louis Godin, Joseph Jussieu, Pierre Bouguer, Jean Godin.*

The names struck a chord: a French scientific expedition, wasn't it, sometime in the eighteenth century? What had they discovered? Not the equator itself, certainly; that had been mapped long before. I asked Antonio. He shrugged and shook his head.

"I don't know, Señorita. Something about the shape of the earth. But that was well before my time. We must go on now if we're to see the market at Otavalo."

My next encounter with the French scientists, a few days later, was in Cuenca, a charming colonial town south of Quito. It's easily explored on foot and I spent some time enjoying the "City of the Four Rivers," with its friendly citizens and its respect for history and tradition. From my travels I have learned that many cities sport the appellation "Athens of . . ."—one to each country, of course. There's Fez in Morocco, Salamanca in Spain, and here Cuenca, the Athens of Ecuador. It has four universities for its one hundred thousand or so inhabitants and a long history of philosophers, musicians, and artists.

There's another side to the traditions of Cuenca, this one not intellectual. I heard about various acts of derring-do and violence in times past. This now peaceful city takes pride in having been described by one of the eighteenth-century governors as "infested with vagrants, gamblers, thieves, and murderers." The hanging post on the outskirts of town attests to punishments, and street boys hurry to point out the exact spot at the door of the Convent of the Conception where "Zavala the Swordsman" met his end.

I was surprised, recalling the sober expressions of the busts at the equator, to learn that one tale concerned the surgeon of the French Expedition, Dr. Seniergues. Here in Cuenca, while the rest of his company recorded the last of their scientific findings, the doctor fell in love with beautiful Manuelita, whom he met on a house call. He squired her around town in the best Parisian manner, to the fury of her previous suitor and the disapproval of church dignitaries. Finally, during an intermission in the bullfight in San Sebastian Plaza, a mob set upon the doctor, pelting him with rocks while spectators yelled, "Death to the French devils!" He died two days later.

I dropped into the state university library and spent an afternoon looking up the history of the town. The name of the French Geodesic Mission kept cropping up, and I was curious enough to take a few notes. The scientists had left France in 1735 on an expedition, sponsored by the French Academy, to take measurements at the equator in order to settle an argument that raged between Jean-Dominique Cassini of the French Academy and Isaac Newton in England. Newton believed the earth to be flattened slightly at the poles and swollen in the middle, causing the planet to wobble like a top, while Cassini was sure that it was lengthened toward the poles and constricted at the equator, as though someone had squeezed it. Who was right?

From my standpoint centuries later, I didn't have to guess;

I knew that Isaac Newton was right. Still, I could understand, as I did my reading, why at that time scientific meetings broke up amid catcalls and insults. National honor was at stake. Who was more intelligent, a Frenchman or an Englishman?

To prove their point, the French launched two expeditions, one to Lapland near the pole and the other to Quito, Peru, close to the equator, to make precise measurements to settle the argument.

The difficulty with Quito was that the Spaniards had always refused permission for foreigners to enter Spain's South American possessions, fearing a breach of the crown's monopoly on New World wealth. However, the French Mission was for the sake of scientific study, not commerce, and the monarchs Philip V of Spain and Louis XV of France were related through the Bourbon line, so it was all in the family. Philip V gave the French Expedition his blessing, also cautiously sending along two Spaniards to make sure that the explorations remained on the up-and-up, with no business transactions.

In Paris, the scientists were lionized. The Mission du Pérou was described by the press as "the greatest expedition the world has known."

Now I began to understand what those scientists were doing in the far reaches of the Andes two hundred and fifty years ago. They started their work at the equator itself, and finished their measurements seven years later, in Cuenca, taking their final observations from the tower of the cathedral. Alas, they turned out to be wrong; Isaac Newton was right and it had to be admitted that the planet, as he maintained, wobbled like a top.

I was about to leave the library when I opened one last book and leafed through its copies of old engravings. There

I came upon the portrait of a woman of the time, Isabel Godin. She had a lovely but solemn face and sat at a desk, holding a folded fan. She looked wealthy and European. I read the faded inscription below the portrait. "Madame Isabel Godin des Odonais, heroine of a terrible journey on the River Amazon."

She must, I supposed, be related to two of the French scientists, Louis and Jean Godin, whose stern busts I had seen at the mitad del mundo. I asked the librarian about her, but he was just closing up on his way home.

"It's an interesting story," he said. "Come in tomorrow and I'll show you the letter her husband, Jean Godin, wrote to Monsieur de La Condamine." He hurried off, calling back over his shoulder, "I'll tell you about the pyramids on the moon, too."

However, early the next morning I was heading back to Quito and thence to Mexico where I live. My holiday was over.

⚜

Back at home I continued to think about the French Geodesic Mission. I had a feeling that I would be meeting people rather than reading impersonal accounts, and I wanted to learn more about them, what they thought and how they lived. As a writer of travel essays, my various wanderings have led me to fascinating places, but I always feel there's something missing: the places are there, but somehow the people escape me. With two and a half centuries between us, it might be impossible to get to know those scientists and their world. Perhaps, however, it would be easier to see them clearly in the distance without the distraction of modern trivia. I was particularly interested in Isabel Godin and the details of her "terrible journey on the River Amazon." While I travel to faraway places I do not, in our modern age, undertake terrible journeys. My interest in this woman already went beyond the ordinary curiosity of a travel writer. I would enjoy doing the research for an article . . . or even a book.

✻

At the library in the Museum of Anthropology in Mexico City I found much material, unknown to me or long forgotten, about the Expedition and its background in history. I continued to make notes of my findings.

The size and shape of the earth interested me from early times. As long ago as 800 B.C. Homer described the earth as a convex disk surrounded by the Oceanus stream, while others believed it to be a round plate supported by four elephants standing on a huge turtle. Scientific knowledge gradually evolved until, in the second century A.D., the roundness of the earth was established. It was an exact sphere, according to Ptolemaic astronomy, its center the center of the universe.

I moved on to the sixteenth century and the Copernican view that the earth travels around the sun and rotates on its own axis, and Isaac Newton's ellipsoidal theory of the earth's measurement, with centrifugal forces causing a flattening of earth at the poles, a bulging at the equator.

These historical facts, if I met them at all, had not stayed with me from school days. I remembered geography as a superlatively boring subject dealing with lists of rivers, countries, states. I adjusted my impression and continued to read.

Jean-Dominique Cassini of the celebrated French Academy of Sciences disagreed with Newton's views. After taking measurements in France he concluded that the earth was flattened not at the poles but at the equator.

I was beginning to see what the Frenchmen had in mind when they arrived in Quito for scientific studies. The question of the exact shape of the earth must be settled. It was essential to determine the roundness of the sphere in order to draw accurate navigational charts. Using maps based on a round earth, navigators had a disconcerting chance of arriving unexpectedly at landfalls; sometimes they even rounded the Horn without knowing it. The length of a longitudinal line from one degree of latitude to the next must be compared with measurements in another latitude.

In sea voyages in the seventeenth and eighteenth centuries, latitude was easily figured with a quadrant by taking sights of the sun or stars, but longitude required the exact time on shipboard to compare with the mean time at Greenwich.

Early proposals for finding longitude at sea were bizarre in the extreme. In England in the seventeenth century it was proposed that a glass filled with water would run over at the instant of a new or full moon. (I couldn't find an explanation for this.) A sailor, according to this theory, could find the exact time, and from that his longitude, twice a month.

From cruises with sailing friends I understood something of navigation in small boats—had even studied it for a while—and had seen the necessity for an accurate chronometer aboard. Sailors at the time of the French Expedition had no accurate timepieces. They depended on crude clocks that never kept good time in the pitching of the ship, the extremes of heat and cold, exposure to spray. They continued to experiment, sometimes leaving a shipboard clock out of it altogether.

One suggestion was to use Sir Kenelm Digby's well-known "powder of sympathy," a cure that was applied to the weapon rather than the wound, leading, according to its proponents, to rapid healing. Following this theory each ship, before leaving England, would be provided with a wounded dog. A reliable observer would be left on shore with an accurate timepiece and a bandage from the dog's wound. Every hour, on the dot, he would dip the dog's bandage in a solution of the powder of sympathy and the dog, on shipboard way out there in the ocean, would accurately yelp the time. No wonder navigators complained that they needed better information.

In March 1714, a petition was submitted to the English Parliament by "several Captains of Her Majesty's Ships, Merchants of London, and Commanders of Merchantmen, setting forth the importance of finding longitude and praying that a public reward be offered for a method of doing it." What was needed, according to Newton, was "a watch to keep time exactly, but by reason of the Motion of a Ship, the variation of Heat and Cold, Wet and Dry, and the Difference of Gravity in different Latitudes, such a Watch hath not yet been made."

A bill was passed "Providing a publick reward for such person or persons as shall discover the Longitude." It had to be determined within thirty nautical miles at the end of a six-weeks' voyage. The prize was the enormous sum of twenty thousand pounds. (I tried to estimate this at today's currency value, but could only compare it to winning the Florida Lottery. Did the Parliament really contemplate paying out such a sum, or were they just hoping that navigators would stop pestering them?) Everybody knew it was impossible to design a clock accurate enough to win the prize. The project provided jokes for the satirists and brought forth a flood of impractical plans.

However, an uneducated Yorkshire carpenter, John Harrison, devoted his life to the project. He developed, over the years, a ticking machine in a box, which he finally refined into a genuine marine chronometer. After he had built five different models, his son set sail to Jamaica to test the final instrument. He encountered a storm that sent the ship off course for days, yet the clock proved amazingly accurate. It lost less than one minute during many months of rough sailing.

Parliament now was obliged, to their surprise and perhaps chagrin, to award the twenty thousand pounds to Harrison. He had been twenty-one years old when the prize was announced; he was seventy-eight when he finally received it.

Eighteenth-century Paris, before the terrors of the Revolution, must have been a splendid place for ambitious, educated young men to live. It was a world center with the latest in architecture—the Élysée Palace, the Palais-Bourbon, the magnificent private homes going up along the Boulevard Saint-Germain. It was a rich city, a city of ostentation and elegance. It was a big city, but a small one for the elite who met each other in the salons, at the theater, or on the tennis courts. There were popular entertainments: variety shows, lotteries, horse races, water-tournaments on the Seine. More important, there was intellectual excitement with the advent of Enlightenment thought, a whole new movement based on the belief that through reason humanity could find knowledge and happiness. The young scientists setting out on the Geodesic Mission must leave all this for an undetermined length of time.

The French Academy of Sciences, founded in 1666, had

become all-powerful in the French scientific world. It organized the "Mission du Pérou," composed of the most learned and adventurous of its members, to explore and make scientific measurements at the equator.

At the head of the Expedition, the Academy placed the renowned astronomer, Louis Godin, accompanied by Pierre Bouguer, astronomer, and Charles-Marie de La Condamine, who combined learning with a flair for publicity and extreme personal ambition. He was an all-around Renaissance man of science. Voltaire spoke of his "burning curiosity" and he was keen to see the New World for himself. He did better than that: by hook or crook, or perhaps bribery, he soon replaced Louis Godin as leader of the Mission. This led later on to much discord.

Besides the three Academicians, the group consisted of Dr. Seniergues, surgeon; Joseph Jussieu, botanist and physician; Hugot, watchmaker; Morainville, technician. Young Couplet, a boy in his teens, nephew of the Academy treasurer, went along for the adventure. Jean Godin, Louis Godin's twenty-one-year-old cousin, signed up as an assistant to the astronomers.

The Expedition members were all young men in their twenties and thirties. (So much for those middle-aged savants portrayed in the busts at the equator.) Each had his own special claim to distinction. Joseph Jussieu, for instance, had become a university professor at the age of fifteen.

Two naval officers, Jorge Juan Santacilla and Antonio de Ulloa, were dispatched from Spain to South America to meet the scientists and keep an eye on them. They were in their early twenties and had attended the naval school at Cadiz, where young Spaniards of noble blood learned to command fleets and govern colonies. They would rendezvous with the

Frenchmen at Cartagena on the northern coast of what is now Colombia. The members of the Geodesic Mission departed from La Rochelle, France, aboard the naval frigate *Portefaix* on May 16, 1735. They loaded aboard a variety of scientific instruments:

two telescopes
one microscope
one Hadley's octant
one "quart de cercle" or quadrant for each scientist, for measuring zenith distances
watches with second hands
compasses with variation

The modern sextant had recently been invented in Philadelphia but apparently the scientists did not have one. Other equipment included:

surveyor's chain and transit
thermometers
barometers
rain gauges
galvanometer
various chemical instruments
an instrument for comparing degrees of blueness of the sky
an instrument to measure the boiling point of water

They took along tools to repair anything that might fall off the pack animals.

The scientists were not simply to study the earth's measurements at the equator. They would combine that with research in various fields, much as astronauts now study all sorts of things as they journey around the world in space. The French Mission resembled space flight, for its members were traveling into what was, for them at least, the unknown.

TWO

Mexico and Boston, Fall 1990

IN MEXICO CITY, I boned up on all I could find about the French Geodesic Mission, the scientists, and life in the eighteenth century. I did not feel that this was a waste of time. I am retired, a stage in life that I think would be better termed *released*—no more pressing responsibilities, no more daily grind—and one of its benefits is waking up in the morning and deciding just what I want to do with my day.

While they are now optional, I still enjoy my former activities: traveling and writing about it. I felt the attraction of a new project here. I would do it at leisure with a background of my years of living and writing. There was the additional hope that the story of Isabel Godin and her "terrible journey," if I could discover enough details about it, would enable me to explore not only fascinating places but a formidable person, a woman for whom travel became a test. This attracted me as a travel writer and as a woman.

I liked reading about the French Mission. I liked to tell people about it, and reactions were different. Some friends changed the subject, but most wanted to pursue it further, especially whatever I could tell them about Isabel Godin and her journey down the Amazon.

Now I proceeded to Boston to visit my sister-in-law and pursue my research.

"You're certainly persistent," she remarked. "Your research has already taken you to Ecuador, Mexico, and the United States. Soon you'll be packing your bags for France."

"Of course not," I laughed. "France is going too far. I'm not a professional historian."

However, I felt a tiny stirring of excitement as I set out for my day at Athenaeum, an elderly, sedate library where I was finding plenty of information to whet and satisfy my appetite.

The Athenaeum is a private library a hundred and fifty years old, housed in a fine old mansion on Beacon Hill. It holds thousands of books, many of them on New England history, but a gratifying number on other subjects. There is a pleasant absence of high-tech equipment and an abundance of interested personnel to help the reader locate books in the open stacks. I was soon able to find my way around without help even in the intricate maze of the basement where treasures gathered dust. To be judged a "rare" book required more than age. I casually took home books that hadn't been checked out for more than a century. I immersed myself in books on eighteenth-century France, early voyages to South America, histories of the Andes and the Amazon basin.

The book I wanted most to read, however, was indeed rare. It contained, along with La Condamine's journal, the letter written by Jean Godin describing in great detail his wife's journey down the Amazon. This letter was the one I had heard about in Cuenca, had failed to find in Mexico, and here it was in New England, remote from its origins. Wonderful! It was dated "Saint-Amand Montrond, Berry, France, 28th July 1773." I hurried to the desk to ask for it.

It was in the rare book room, a locked sanctum full of who knows what treasures. It was treated with suitable respect. First I was seated at a table in view of employees, urged to surrender my ballpoint pen in favor of a pencil, given as a bookmark a special kind of string with a weight on the end to hold the pages open. Then a pad of handsome mauve velvet was set before me with bolsters of the same shade on each side of it. The book—it did look somewhat the worse for wear, but what can be expected after more than two hundred years?—was laid carefully on the mat, its covers opened to lie on the bolsters, and I was left to my find.

Soon I was immersed in a real-life story rivaling any fiction: Isabel Godin, a girl of Riobamba, Peru, was married at thirteen to the youngest of the visiting French scientists, Jean Godin. Unable to go down the Amazon with him when he set out to return to France, she waited twenty years, dreaming of reunion with her husband and a new life in Europe. Amazingly, word finally came. She then set out with her two brothers and a group of retainers to cross the entire continent of South America, following the rivers to the mouth of the Amazon. Misfortunes dogged the travelers until, lost in the jungle, starving, exhausted, all of them died—all except Isabel. She wandered for nine days in the trackless forest, was rescued by Indians, set on her way again downriver, and eventually joined her husband. Together they reached Jean Godin's home city of Saint-Amand Montrond in France, lived there for many years, and are still remembered for their adventures.

I read the long letter several times, making notes, then asked for a photocopy. This was regretfully refused for fear of injury to the book's already weak spine. I learned of a duplicate at the Harvard library, however, and obtained a copy of that.

That night I lay awake thinking of the long-ago adventurers. I wanted to learn more about Isabel Godin. Even in the little I had read, her character came through. She was a heroine, though probably she did not consider herself one. She was a natural leader and intrepid adventurer. Hers was a great love story: waiting twenty years for a reunion with her husband, the equivalent of Penelope's wait for Odysseus. She must have been socially broad-minded; she studied the Quechua language for the pleasure of it while other eighteenth-century ladies of fashion were looking down on the Indians and their culture.

When I finally went to sleep, my dreams were confusing. I wandered through a trackless forest—not the Amazon basin, however, but more like the New England woods in the country where I grew up. Those friendly Indians in my dream wore the feather headdresses of the Mohawks. Reading about them years ago had been one of the first occasions when I had an inkling that there was more in the world than my suburban neighborhood and that I would like to explore that world.

Paris, with its academy, and the city of Saint-Amand Montrond, south of there, had begun to attract me. Not so far away now, with speedy nonstop flights. First, though, I wanted to return to Ecuador, to Quito and Riobamba, to look for more details about the scientists and about Isabel and Jean Godin.

THREE

Ecuador, November 1990

AS SOON AS I had leisure and funds for such a journey, I returned to Ecuador. This part of South America was interesting me more and more. I could easily get into the habit of flying down to Quito, not difficult from Mexico City where one climbs aboard in the evening, spends a more or less uneasy night trying to sleep, and rouses at dawn to see the sun rising over lofty, snow-covered peaks, some of which belch smoke and steam. It is a superb way to get a view of these icy giants of the Andes—Chimborazo, Pichincha, Cotopaxi—jutting up through the low-hanging clouds. Over the centuries they have inspired extravagant literary descriptions, none more glowing than that of Lieutenant Charles Brand of the English Royal Navy, who came to Quito in 1827.

"Oh, Man," he wrote, "If ever thou hast the vanity to think thyself more than thou really art, a mere worm upon the earth, or that thou art superior to any other of thy fellow-worms crawling here below—go, in the depth of winter, and view the tremendous cordillera."

The lieutenant had no opportunity to see those mountains from the air. If he had, might he have equated us with something more lowly than a worm?

There can be no more impressive plane landing in the world than that at Quito, a city tucked in the bottom of a valley nine thousand feet up, surrounded by mountains. On the edge of town is a small landing field. It looks too small. The plane circles once or twice. Passengers hold their breaths, and perhaps the pilot holds his, then we swoop down to land with a roaring of brakes. Is there room to come to a stop? Yes, just, but not room for dignified deceleration. I breathe a sigh of relief before gathering up my bundles for debarking.

The members of the Geodesic Mission, arriving at Quito in 1736, were suitably impressed, not only with the mountains but with the city snuggled among them. Crossing a high pass between the summits of Pichincha and Cotopaxi, La Condamine looked down in amazement at a white city in the valley below. He wrote in his journal:

"Arrived at the height and was seized with astonishment mixed with admiration, at sight of a valley five or six leagues long and cut into by streams that joined to form a river. There were cultivated fields, little hamlets, greenery. I thought myself transported into our most beautiful provinces of France. As I descended I passed by degrees from extreme cold to the temperature of a fine May day. I saw flowers, buds and fruits on trees; sowing, cultivating and harvesting all at one day and in the same place."

Jorge Juan, one of the Spanish officers, in his own account of this historic journey, gave a careful description of Quito. It was the size of a second-class European city, he noted, with country houses and cultivated land round about. The climate? Eternal spring. In the main square of Quito were impressive buildings: the cathedral, the government building, the Episcopal Palace. (They are still there.) There was a beautiful fountain in the center of the square.

However, the city streets were in sorry shape, running up, down, and sideways, some of them entirely ruined or with troops of cattle stampeding through. The buildings had small windows to keep out the wind and even the principal streets were unpaved. There wasn't a single civilized vehicle or carriage in the city. The men strode down the streets with servants holding parasols over their heads. The women were carried everywhere by sedan chair.

The air of the city was full of the cries of wild asses, the lowing of cattle, and the bleating of lambs, while the constant breeze carried the fragrance of chirimoyas, avocados, and cheese along with the stench of open sewers.

The next day I go again to the mitad del mundo and study the busts. They do not flatter the Frenchmen. Jean Godin does not look like a young, eager suitor, hurrying to Riobamba to court the beautiful thirteen-year-old Isabel. He looks like a Supreme Court justice.

The sight of a group of Indians, North American Indians, draws my attention from the busts. Their splendid bright feather headdresses look just like the ones I tried to copy from a picture book when I was ten years old and had access to turkey feathers. These can't be descendants of the Incas. Questioning their leader, I learn that they are of the Winnebago tribe, come all the way from Wisconsin to hold today, November 1, the Indian solstice, a ceremony to invoke world peace. They will have their service standing on the exact center of the world.

This time I have come out by bus and can wander leisurely around the area, where there are several small buildings. One is marked "French Pavilion," but I do not know what it holds. The door is locked, the place apparently deserted. The custodian of the building nearby tells me he has no idea where the French went or when they will return, if ever. He shows me his own exhibit, a model replica of the city of Quito in the eighteenth century. It fills a whole room, each tiny building a reproduction meticulously to scale, each street labeled, each church named.

"Now we'll see Quito at night." The guard turns off the ceiling lights in this windowless room and presses a switch. Suddenly, colonial Quito is illuminated from within, as though each three-hundred-year-old house were again inhabited, each church crowded with worshippers buttressing their religious faith in a newfound land. Isabel Godin might be here, up for a fiesta from her Riobamba home, escorted by her husband Jean.

The custodian sells me a large, colored plan of old Quito and I return to the city. Much of old Quito still exists, balanced by the new city of high-rise buildings and broad boulevards that abuts it, testifying to the riches of oil found in the jungle.

Back in Quito I wander around the old city, imagining myself there at the time of the French Expedition. Architecturally this part of Quito hasn't changed much, I suppose, except that the streets are now paved and I don't see any Spanish gentlemen walking in the shade of parasols held aloft by servants, or ladies wending their way in sedan chairs to the day's engagements. The dense modern traffic proceeds one-way through the maze of narrow ancient streets.

Pedestrians mingle with it, for street vendors, hawking everything from brassieres to Bibles, have proliferated until there is no room to use the sidewalks. I have just visited the archives and am passing the cathedral on my way to a bookstore when I notice that the street is unusually full of people. The rush hour perhaps. I am wedged in among a group of young men, women, and children who seem determined not to let me go on my way.

It's a moment or two before I realize that I have been robbed. While his older brothers hugged me close, a small boy has deftly slashed my camera bag with a razor blade. They have all vanished instantly into the crowd.

Fortunately there's not too much lost. My passport is back at the hotel; my money, except for a small sum now in the little boy's possession, is secreted on my person. My camera was too big to pull from its bag. Well, "ni modo," as we say in Mexico, I'll be on my way. However, I am again halted, this time by well-wishers. A woman with a baby, an old man, and two teenaged girls hurry to my assistance.

"You have been robbed. Are you hurt? Can we help you?"

I explain that the loss was minor, but they are determined to assist me.

"We'll get you a taxi to your hotel."

"No," I explain, "I must change some money first."

So we all proceed to the nearest money changers, where I am treated with great sympathy and revived with an orange crush. My money is changed and I am sent out with two bodyguards to hail a taxi. Everyone has agreed on an explanation of the incident.

"Of course they weren't Ecuadoreans. They must have come across the border from Colombia."

When I get back to my hotel, the desk clerk spots the rip in my bag.

"Another one," he says, shaking his head, "it happens all the time." He hands me my room key. "Of course," he adds, "they were Colombians."

Meantime, I have hired Señor Vega, the taxi man who drove me to the hotel, to take me on a longer trip tomorrow.

※

I am headed the next day for Riobamba where Isabel lived and where she married Jean. It's a three-hour drive south of Quito along the Avenue of Volcanoes. These rear up, just as they did two hundred and fifty years ago, awe-inspiring, threatening—Cochibamba, Tungurahua, Altar, smoking Sangay. My driver points out and names the peaks. "This is the Avenue of the Volcanoes," he says, and I know that it is also a section of the Pan-American Highway. I remark on this to Señor Vega.

"Of course," he says. He is a short man of middle age, thin, a bit worried, his thick glasses a little too big for his nose. He looks remarkably like Mr. Burch, the high school math teacher who used to keep us all in our places.

"It's a long way to Riobamba," he remarks, pressing down on the gas pedal.

The highway runs alongside jagged cliffs, above which the volcanoes tower. Clouds march leisurely across a gray-blue sky that, up here in the altiplano at ten thousand feet, seems broader than in the lowlands, an almost limitless canopy, spread high above the wide plain that separates the mountains. The landscape is geometrical, with fields oblong or square divided by groups of dark green sentinel pines, lines of knifelike maguey cactus, and feathery clumps of pampas grass. There are signs of civilization, many of them the same ones that Isabel would have seen: on the mountain slopes almost vertical cultivated fields in strong colors of emerald green, mahogany, and tan with black-and-white cows loitering in them. White adobe houses with red tile roofs squat among the eucalyptus trees (trees not yet imported when the French were here). The cottages are small, with wooden fretwork carved in lacy patterns along the eaves and good-luck crosses perched on the rooftrees.

In the time of the French Expedition, the scant traffic must have consisted of men on horseback, Indians herding llamas, and, when weather permitted, the occasional carriage jouncing its way from Quito to the rural city of Riobamba where, it was said, the lives of the rich landowners were more sophisticated than in the capital itself.

Today the traffic is heavy. It is November 2, All Souls' Day. Important in Mexico, in Ecuador it is even more so. Today and tomorrow all business stops. The country is on holiday, not, as in Mexico, a strange almost merry celebration, but one of somber thoughts. Families gather to speak sadly of the dead and to take flowers to their graves.

In the dense holiday traffic, policemen are stationed every few kilometers to supervise the orderly flow of cars. Half the population of Quito is heading south to join relatives in Riobamba, Baños, or Cuenca, while the population of those cities hurries to the capital.

My driver lights a Full Speed cigarette and we pass a truck with "Condor" scrawled in big letters on its side. Small, brightly colored, crowded buses zip along, weaving in and out—"The Warrior of Love," says one. A family is gathered by the highway building a fire, with a large pig ready to roast. We pass some cyclists pedaling as though late for a race, or perhaps they are already in a race. An Indian trudges along in the opposite direction, his bicycle balanced on his head.

While Señor Vega battles the traffic hazards, I think about

this highway, picturing it as it must have looked in Inca times centuries ago. There would have been constant traffic across the high plain. This was the main route north to Quito from Cuzco, some seven hundred miles to the south. The Inca emperor took this way each year for the annual survey of his huge kingdom. Crowds accompanied him, carrying everything for his comfort and pleasure. Emperor Huayna Capac, for instance, set forth on a journey that would take months, with two thousand women, twenty-five thousand llamas, and multitudes of followers to provide for his wants. One of the greatest of Inca rulers, he preferred the north country to the capital at Cuzco. Along this very track, as it was then in the early sixteenth century, chasquis, or royal messengers, ran in relays to herald his arrival as he proceeded in his gold-and feather-trimmed litter.

I look out the window for a while. We pass billboards: Marlboro, Texaco, Pepsi, Coca-Cola. Señor Vega almost collides with a truck full of alfalfa as he turns to point out a small rabbitlike animal running alongside us, apparently trying to outstrip the cars.

"Guasache," he says.

I look with interest at what appears to be a cross between a rabbit and a squirrel. Then it disappears into a bush and I go on with my thoughts, hoping Señor Vega will not endanger us by seeing anything more of interest along the highway.

I am thinking about the Spanish travelers who must have come by this road, also in the sixteenth century, during the time of Huayna Capac. They were not many in number, only two hundred or so, but they had supernatural powers. They traveled by sea in great wooden houses, carried long sticks that spouted thunderbolts, appeared on four-legged animals that may even have been part of them. Most convincing of all, as the emperor's spies reported, "the lions and wild animals in your palace at Tombes crouched to the ground before them and wagged their tails."

The Spaniards did, of course, defeat the Incas even though it was two hundred against millions. Firearms and cavalry prevailed, as did the plague brought by the invaders, an epidemic of smallpox that killed thousands. A civil war slaughtered thousands more. And their superstitious fears made the Indians easy victims.

So the Lord-Inca Huayna Capac never came this way again to inspect his kingdom and receive his subjects' homage. But the Spanish conquerors soon had their own misfortunes. They had their share of superstitions, fairy tales that led them to go bravely into an unexplored wilderness from which they returned—those who did return—in pitiable condition.

"Shall we stop here?" Señor Vega parks at a corner store selling sandwiches and cuy—guinea pigs roasted on spits. They look sadly vulnerable and I am not hungry. Leaving Señor Vega to his midmorning snack, I walk a little way down a side road, unpaved, winding among the fields. I meet two women in Indian costume trudging briskly toward the highway, perhaps to catch a bus for a family reunion. They are spinning as they walk, twisting the threads industriously onto the spindles. This seems to take the place of conversation, for they don't speak to each other, or to me as we pass, although they smile. On the way back to the highway I watch several hummingbirds shooting by toward Tungurahua Volcano where I suppose they nest. I recall the fanciful Inca names for these birds, of which there are a couple of hundred varieties in Ecuador: Sun Angels, Violet Ears, Green Hermits.

Back on the highway, while Señor Vega maneuvers with

refreshed zeal among the buses, motorcycles, trucks, and ancient family sedans, I think about the Spaniards who came this way almost four hundred years ago—a cortege as impressive as the Inca's retinue, and rivaling the procession of Toyotas and Fords on this Day of the Dead.

Their lure was profit, for which they came to a savage continent, and the "Land of Cinnamon" they believed would provide it. So far, Portuguese interests had controlled the spices of the Far East; this new supply would cut them down to size. Gonzalo Pizarro, heading south from Quito, intended to find this cinnamon country of which he had heard. He left the city in February 1541 with a band of two hundred soldiers on horseback, each with his bag of provisions, his gun, and ammunition. Everything else was carried by "inferiors." There were four thousand Indian slaves, two thousand hogs for food, a great line of pack animals, and two thousand enormous savage hunting dogs to subdue hostile tribes and keep the Indian slaves in order. The dogs could be eaten if supplies ran short.

The party soon met difficulties—forests where horses could not penetrate, rain that soaked the riders and their equipment. When they finally reached the Land of Cinnamon, they found the trees of no use to them. The leaves had the flavor, but not the bark from which the spice is made. Their return journey to Quito was a nightmare. Zarate, a historian of the time, tells us, "Pizarro returned back again to Quito, from whence he had travelled more than four hundred leagues of evil way . . . where forty of his men ended their days . . . even as they asked for meat, they fell down dead with hunger. . . . They killed their horses which were left, and greyhounds with other sort of dogs to eat." Other chroniclers reveled in horror stories: Pizarro's men bled their horses once a week and used their helmets to cook up a meal of blood and herbs. Then they turned to lizards, frogs, and roots. . . . Finally they were eating nothing but leather belts and soles of shoes. Toward the end of the journey, the explorers died at the rate of four to a mile.

I prefer to think of Pizarro and his men when they started their journey, marching away from Quito, banners flying, horses prancing. I imagine the thousands of Indians, the hundreds of horses, the dogs and pigs and lines of pack animals, and the dense crowd of onlookers watching a party of adventurers proceeding jauntily into the unknown.

Señor Vega leans on the horn. We come to a jouncing halt behind an oxcart covering the distance at its accustomed speed. It's a few moments before we find a traffic opening where we can get around it, although Señor Vega continues to ply the horn relentlessly.

"Not much further to Riobamba," he says, as we gather speed again. "We'll be there in time for lunch."

There are a number of rivers and streams to cross and I wonder, consulting the detailed map that I bought in Quito, which one is the Bobonaza, that headwater of the distant Amazon. The name of the town in the Oriente where Isabel started her canoe travel on the Bobonaza River was, I recall, Canelos, "City of Cinnamon Trees." Had she thought before starting on her journey of the horrors the Spanish had suffered in that country two hundred years before?

The members of the French Expedition were well aware, in the enlightened eighteenth century, of the historical interest of their Mission du Pérou. Several of them kept journals with a view to publication. Splitting up into groups, they spent a total of seven years surveying a line from the equator to Cuenca, some three hundred kilometers to the south, in order to map the exact distance from one parallel of latitude to the next along a meridian of longitude. This was referred to as "measuring the arc." Difference in these measurements between the pole and the equator would indicate a difference in the shape of the earth. Because of the difficult mountain terrain (did they know about this when they planned the Expedition, I wonder?), it was a mammoth task to make even the simplest topographic measurements. They spent much of their seven years climbing peaks and signaling to each other, working out the complicated details needed for their triangulations. Besides, each of the scientists had his own specialty to which he devoted what time he could spare from measuring the arc. Jussieu collected plant specimens to be sent to the Jardin des Plantes in Paris. Bouguer studied the heavens for new stars and planets. La Condamine considered native remedies, quinine for instance. They had plenty of time to study this part of the world, to experience its trials and pleasures.

Antonio de Ulloa, one of the Spanish officers, described in his journal what living was like in a small cabin at a high altitude:

"We stayed ordinarily in the cabin, as much because of the cold and violent winds, as because we were customarily wrapped in a cloud so thick that we couldn't see distinctly an object at a distance of seven or eight feet. . . . When the clouds were raised, their density made breathing difficult, snow . . . fell continuously in great flakes, and violence of the winds made us apprehensive of any movement, seeing ourselves carried away with our habitations and thrown into some abyss to be soon buried in ice and snow." When they came down from the mountains "the cabins of the Indians and the cow stables on the side of the mountains looked to us like palaces; rough villages seemed opulent cities, the conversations of the priest and two or three people within seemed a speech of Plato."

Cold was the chief hazard the scientists had to face in their lightweight tents at altitudes of fifteen thousand feet and more. Everyone had a chafing dish of hot coals in his tent, over which he held his plate of boiled rice and fowl to keep it from freezing as he ate. "Our lips swelled and chapped," Jorge Juan wrote, "so that every motion, of speech or the like, drew blood." La Condamine wrote of being lost in a storm, abandoned by his guide, clinging to his mule for warmth, losing the feeling in his feet as they started to freeze, and warming them with his urine.

Here, on the Avenue of the Volcanoes, in the year 1990, driving along a well-paved highway, I look up at the volcanoes as we pass them, and can only imagine what camping on their summits must have been like. Here the sun has come out and the roadway heats up. "Eternal spring," I think, turning into "temporary summer." We have passed through Latacunga and Ambato. The map tells me that Riobamba should be next. As we cross a stream, its flow meager at this end of the dry season, I wonder again about the Bobonaza. Might that have been it, or at least its origins, before it grew into the river where Isabel journeyed? The Pastaza starts around here, too. Later, when we're not bowling along, I'll see if I can disentangle the thin blue lines running among the volcanoes on my map, to discover the river that, farther down when it had found its power, led Isabel almost to her death.

I ask Señor Vega to stop the car when we come to a widening in the highway. The stream meanders beside us. Looking surprised and not too approving, he does so.

"Only for a moment, Señorita," he remarks. After all, who is driving this car? I feel reprimanded.

"Just a moment. That is what I meant."

"Riobamba is where you asked me to go. At least fifteen

kilometers from here. There is nothing around here."

There is, in fact, nothing except the stream in sight, along with a view of high plains and pastureland, and Tungurahua looming in the distance.

"I am looking for the Bobonaza River. This is probably it."

I will be content with finding the quiet beginnings of the river. Here it is a narrow, innocent-looking stream with bushes of yellow broom growing beside it, wandering through the fields gathering strength as melting snow from the mountains feeds it. Isabel may have come here with her brothers to picnic. She must have crossed it when her party left on muleback for their great adventure.

"Yes, of course this is it," Señor Vega says, "but it's not much of a river. Actually it may be the Pastaza; they are just alike." He revs up the motor.

"Wait a minute," I say. I get out and take a photograph showing what? Only a small stream rippling over pebbles in a green field where half a dozen holsteins graze and the eucalyptus trees murmur in a light breeze. The Bobonaza—I have decided this is it—is starting its long progress through gorges and over waterfalls, down, down from the altiplano to the jungle country of the Oriente, the land of dense green torrid forests, savage vines, thirty-foot serpents, and deadly insects too small to see.

Along with these perils, eighteenth-century travelers faced, if plans went wrong, a loss of direction—the jungle is terribly, monotonously the same—then thirst, starvation, gradual abandonment of hope, and the final, inevitable jungle terror, espanto de la selva. That is how a group of wanderers perished, all of them except Isabel. How did she survive?

We presently arrive at Riobamba, a town of about fifty thousand, dominated by its church, which looks over the main square. In the square is a lofty column topped by a statue of Pedro Vicente Maldonado, friend of Isabel's family, who went with La Condamine down the Amazon. The town has not forgotten its history, although I know that the Riobamba of the 1730s was completely destroyed by an earthquake in 1797. It was rebuilt half a dozen miles away in the same colonial style of white walls and red tile roofs.

Riobamba is noted for its view of Tungurahua Volcano flanked by Altar and smoking Sangay, the three peaks jutting up to the east. Rows of palm trees line the wide streets, almost empty today since everyone is at the cemetery. The pharmacy is locked and the Panaderia Jésus de Gran Poder, at the corner, is closed, although a fragrance of baking bread drifts out.

The tourist office is closed tight, as is the museum, where I might find relics or mementos of the Frenchmen. No use staying until tomorrow, for that, too, is the Day of the Dead (one day for adults, one for children). After that, the weekend when nothing will be open. I may as well give up on research here. It's more than two hundred and fifty years since Isabel grew up in Riobamba and the Frenchmen arrived there for their surveys. The families of those days have probably died out, forgotten the past, or lost interest in a distant ancestor who married a foreigner and went east all the way to Paris, a world away.

I do have good luck in Quito, locating two slim volumes about international meetings held there, one on the two hundredth anniversary of the French Mission, the other as recently as 1986, on the two hundred and fiftieth. If I'd known, I'd have been there. I buy the books and read them with interest. Dignitaries presided and scholars gave speeches. France sent notable members of the Academy as well as statesmen. These books give detailed histories of the work of the Expedition and its findings. They include chapters on Isabel Godin's journey on the Amazon but little personal detail. The speeches are quoted at length in all their stilted prose. They seem to be speaking of the Roman busts at the mitad del mundo.

Señor Vega and I eat our sandwiches in the main plaza, sitting on a bench facing the church. A few mourners, most of them women in black, come out and walk purposefully through the square intent on where they are going. I notice a faint odor of incense, and a distant church bell calls worshippers in some other part of town.

It's a long drive back to Quito and Señor Vega is impatient to get started. I take one more circuit on foot around the square and along the surrounding streets. There is a sign set into the door of a modern building. Looking closer I read the words "Instituto Tecnico Isabel Godin." I peer through the window but can't see much in the dark interior. There seem to be big commercial sewing machines, the furnishings of a factory. So the Frenchmen, or at least a heroine of the time, are still remembered here. Too bad that I can't stay until Monday to see the factory in operation, perhaps get valuable information.

On the way back to Quito there is a side road leading off to Baños, a watering place where Isabel Godin stopped on her journey.

"Let's go there," I suggest hopefully, "and from there we could go on to Canelos . . . , " but Señor Vega shakes his head vigorously and explains. Certainly not. Baños is easy to get to but uninteresting, and the road to Canelos would be the death of his taxi. Reading my current map, I see that there really is no road marked to Canelos, only the note, "projected highway." Two hundred and fifty years have brought few changes. I will have to live with the details I already have.

Back in Mexico I look through my notes and consider what I have accomplished. The city of Quito is familiar to me now, as is Riobamba. Cuenca I visited during my previous trip. The volcanoes on which the scientists spent those rugged years are best viewed from a distance. No need to climb them. My imagination can conjure up the perils and I want no part of that.

The high plateau where Isabel grew up is beautiful but remote. No wonder she dreamed of travel beyond the volcanoes to whatever she would find there—the jungle, the great river, the ocean, and Paris itself.

I have done enough reading now to be sure that I want to go on with my research. Best to begin at the beginning and follow the Expedition from its start. The French Academy of Sciences must be full of information, worth the long trip to find it. I call the local travel agent.

"Please book me a flight for Paris," I tell her.

FOUR

Mexico and Paris, 1991

MY PLANE TICKET IS reserved, and I have written to a small hotel on Paris's Left Bank to expect me. Then I wake up one night with qualms about the Academy. Can an ordinary member of the public, and a foreigner at that, ring the bell and walk right in? Consultation with a friend who has done research in Paris tells me that, of course, they cannot.

"Very few people get in," she tells me. "Why don't you consult the French embassy in Mexico City?"

I do so, carrying a description of my project and an explanation of why I need to see original documents. It's not as hard as my friend thought.

"This will get you in," the cultural attaché says kindly, handing me a scribbled note on embassy paper beginning *Cher André.* "We are always happy to help anyone interested in French history."

So I start out armed with a letter from the attaché to the permanent secretary of the French Academy of Sciences.

I have a few more qualms. Many years ago, too many, I

spent a year in Paris studying at the Sorbonne. I can still read and understand the language if it is delivered at a reasonable speed, but how about speaking it after all this time? I wake up early each morning to turn on a linguistic tape, but the real thing will be different, under pressure, with someone looking impatiently at me for an answer. My biggest problem is my more recent knowledge of Spanish. My sentences frequently begin in French and end in Spanish. Well, they're both Latin languages, aren't they?

I make my final preparations and climb aboard the Air France direct flight from Mexico City to Paris. It's a journey of ten hours or so, enough time to think over my plans, perhaps even regret them. I am more or less reversing the route taken by the frigate *Portefaix* in 1735. The ship was at sea for thirty-seven days as it breasted the waves and the passengers counted the weeks until they would make landfall. There must have been much to watch even in a lonely ocean: seabirds, flying fish, approaching rain squalls, the cresting of waves in a high wind, and the luffing of sails on calm days.

My own journey is brief, but it seems long in the absence of any excitement except the serving of a meal or two and the showing of a movie. No view from the window, just a plateau of clouds. I think back to when I came this way many years ago, over the Atlantic Ocean, not above it. It was by passenger ship (the *Rotterdam*? I'm not sure of the name now) and I remember that the voyage was excitingly fast— New York to Cherbourg in a mere five and a half days. Hardly time to get one's sea legs and meet one's fellow passengers. My thoughts then may have approximated Isabel's when she set out from Riobamba—a chance to explore beyond the volcano, to see the world. I was young and my destination was Paris!

Now, peering out the plane window, I see only those drifting banks of cloud. The movie is finished; it's time to sleep, but I am wakeful, thinking about my plans and how they may turn out. What will I find in the French archives? Maybe nothing of interest, perhaps my trip will be a waste of time. Decidedly I should have prepared better—at least written in advance. There may be nothing in Paris I could not have found in the big libraries at home. In that case I'll put on a show for my friends when I get back. I'll make up exciting incidents if necessary to justify my obsession with a long-ago scientific expedition and Isabel Godin's disastrous journey. I'll hint at thrilling discoveries.

Maybe, though, there will be some worthwhile findings. . . . No, not likely after all these years. I have only a slim hope of finding original letters and records, not to speak of living descendants. I'll take what comes and view this trip as a nostalgic return to my months in Paris half a century ago.

I fall asleep just in time to be wakened for breakfast and an imminent landing.

Paris seems to have changed little over the years, at least in the downtown area. The same gray color hangs in the sky and tinges the ancient buildings. There are no strident colors here. Paris may be the only city where gray is beautiful. The river flows along as always, carrying barge-loads of passengers oohing and aahing at the towers of Notre Dame and the hazy spike of the Eiffel Tower.

After checking in at my hotel, where the manager's relentless English makes civilized French impossible, I go for a walk, fighting jet lag, along the Left Bank. Not much change here. The booksellers are in their old places—must be the booksellers' sons by now—but the old laundry barge has disappeared, rotted away, or has been superseded by laundromats. The traffic along the Left Bank is dense but perfectly controlled. Without consciously intending to, I follow the Quais in the direction of the Academy. There it is, rising majestically beside the river. Its huge dome makes me think of an enormous cranium filled with important knowledge. The Académie des Sciences, one of the five Academies, where my information lies, must be somewhere inside the imposing building. I'll sleep off the effects of eight hours' time change, then get started on my undertaking.

It is extremely hot in Paris this July. The city is experiencing what the newspapers refer to as the worst canicule (dog days) of the century. There are photos of vineyards pathetically dry, the land cracked open. I, too, feel the effect of one-hundred-degree temperature in this small hotel that has no aspirations toward air-conditioning. Running cold water over my wrists is helpful, and I abandon all thoughts of modesty with my bedroom door open to attract a stray draft. Still, it is a dog night.

In the morning, revived by hot café au lait and rolls, I head determinedly along the Quais again toward the Academy, only a little apprehensive, with the "Cher André" letter clutched in my hand.

The courtyard is vast and the court behind it must be even larger. A sign points to the entrance, an archway that I approach with caution. Yes, of course, it is guarded. A soldier, or other uniformed caretaker, materializes from a guardroom, and simply bars my way, frowning. Looking back on it, I think he had a gun, but perhaps he only acted like a guard with a gun. I proffer my "Cher André" letter and smile hopefully.

It takes three careful readings for the guard to be convinced that I offer no threat to French learning, that all is comme il faut, propre, and convenable. He motions me in, without a smile, and retreats back to his den.

Now I am standing in a big inner courtyard. There are no arrows, signs, or other directions to the doors opening on all sides from it. The place seems to be empty. I wander for a few moments, trying to look sure of myself, ready to go into the first open door. Suddenly two gentlemen appear beside me, affable and courteous. What can they do to help?

Feeling a little shy, I offer the "Cher André" letter, which is read with interest by the older of the two men. His clothes, his manner, and his speech all somehow tell me that he is not a lowly employee. He waves a hand toward the far left corner of the courtyard and delivers a cannon-round of French. I do catch the words Académie des Sciences, so that must be where it is. He hands my letter to the other gentleman, who reads it with attention. "Ah, a letter from Mexico." He gives it back to me and I walk between my new acquaintances, who have evidently decided to escort me to my destination, talking all the way. Why do Frenchmen have to talk so fast? What shall I say? Better a silent American, I decide, than an American speaking bad French.

"I understand French," I tell them, carefully choosing from my simple vocabulary, "but I have not been here for many years so I can no longer speak it."

The older man—can it possibly be the permanent secretary, "André" himself?—opens a door ceremoniously and ushers me into a room.

"The archives," he says. "This is what you want, Mademoiselle. When you return to Mexico, give my regards to my friends at the embassy. And do not worry. You cannot speak

French, but you do understand it, and that at least is something."

The archives are in a simple square room, shady and fairly cool, with a table in the middle and chairs enough for eight or ten readers. There were never that many there during the month when I haunted the place. The walls are lined, not with shelves, but with built-in drawers, big ones that open on hinged flaps to reveal the treasures behind them. These documents, since they are all shapes and sizes, are packed into filing folders and tied with cloth tapes so that the reader can open them and go through the randomly filed contents, return them to their folders, and hand back the fat file to one of the archivists, who returns it to its drawer. It is a simple, effective way to lose nothing, for the drawer stays open until the file is returned to it and a glance at the wall shows which are in use.

An archivist greets me and shows me to a seat.

The drawers are labeled in enormous letters: "Balzac," "Diderot," "Voltaire." Among them I find the caches for Charles-Marie de La Condamine, Pierre Bouguer, Joseph Jussieu. My friends are all here. I hand my "Cher André" letter, which is getting a little rumpled, to the archivist and sit down at the table, where there are three other readers. One is an old man whose white beard threatens to get stuck in the file he is studying. Another, an eager-looking Asian, Japanese perhaps, flips skillfully through a mass of notes. I figure him for a student the day before an exam. The third, at the end of the table, is a mysterious-looking woman in black. She is poring over an open file, seeming never to turn the pages. Ah, a real mystery woman, researching some juicy scandal among her ancestors, a death by treachery, the stealing of a scientific finding by an unscrupulous Academy member.

She looks up and gives me a smile, and the mystery vanishes. She's just someone like me looking up an interesting past.

I mention La Condamine to the archivist, who nods understandingly and hands back my André letter.

"Il y a beaucoup de choses," she murmurs, opening the proper drawer and heaving down two thick files tied up with lengths of yellow tape. "I hope you have some time, Mademoiselle. We are open from ten to three."

"I have plenty of time," I say, returning to her the card that I have made out to show my identity, address, and the object of my studies. "I have a month."

I untie the tapes and spread the first folder flat on the table. It is full of handwritten notes on scraps of paper, printed pamphlets and newspaper clippings, letters written in a spidery hand. Now I see what will be my greatest difficulty. Another problem I did not consider beforehand: the difficulty of reading eighteenth-century handwriting in the language and script of that time, some of it clear enough, some faded with the centuries. Well, I have a month to do it. I start my research at random, for the file is not sorted by date or subject matter. Almost at once I am absorbed, transported in a way that never seemed possible, to another place, another time, a different world.

It is now time, as I go along, to make some order of my notes and my thoughts. Here I can follow the Frenchmen from the inception of their enterprise, across the ocean, into the mountains, and later home again. The writing is not really that hard to read, and there is no problem with the printed material, just the *s*'s masquerading as *f*'s and the formal convoluted style. Here, for instance, is a list of personal possessions carried by the group:

medicines

books

12 shotguns

6 sabers

11 fencing swords

255 pounds of gunpowder

9 barrels of French brandy

surgical instruments

28 suits of clothes

bags of powder for dressing wigs

So far, so good. I can picture the members of the Expedition arriving at La Rochelle, the port on the west coast of France, each with his portmanteau, his hampers, his trunk of necessaries, and his carefully wrapped scientific instruments.

La Condamine was a man of middle age, as age was counted in those chancy times—thirty-four—sophisticated, with travel and experience of the world. Histories differ as to his appearance, some reporting that he was a small man, almost a dwarf, and that his face was so scarred from smallpox that he hesitated to appear at social gatherings. Other contemporary accounts give a different picture, of a man adept in social circles, a lady's man, even a womanizer, who delighted the salons with his witty verses. Whichever was the case, everyone agreed that he was a man of burning ambition, making the most of any opportunity for publicity. Nowhere did I find a definitive explanation of how he became the leader of the Expedition, even though Louis Godin had been appointed its head. Whatever the means, bribery or influence at headquarters, it was no way to start a peaceful, cooperative association of scientists. In fact, after a while, Godin and La Condamine quit talking to each other entirely and each carried on his experiments and calculations independently.

Joseph Jussieu was known to be a prodigy of learning, becoming a university professor at the early age of fifteen (he was now thirty-two), but he was considered to be eccentric and a bit unstable. So I was not surprised to read, at the top of a page of scribbled unsigned notes, that Jussieu, there in the harbor before the frigate even sailed, hid in a locker aboard and had to be found and placated. The note said he was bitten by a vicious . . . ? What? I could not make out the scrawl. It seemed to begin with the letter *m* and go on for four or five scribbled letters. Whatever it was, it was the property of Bouguer, who had brought it aboard, and Jussieu was deeply upset.

I tried in vain to solve the enigma. The archivists were unable to help—they couldn't read the word either. The Asian student had already hurried away, his notebook clutched firmly, to some all-important deadline. The lady in black—maybe she was just a little mysterious—merely smiled politely and shook her head as she gazed at the word. The old man with the beard had fallen asleep, his head pillowed by a folder of letters.

It was not essential for me to know what bit Joseph Jussieu as the frigate *Portefaix* prepared to sail in 1735. But what could it have been? Certainly not a dog . . . chien does not begin with an *m*, nor does bouledogue or caniche, "poodle," nor any other breed of dog I could find in my dictionary. What else? I woke in the night wondering. Of course, it didn't really matter, but still . . . what? Did Bouguer have a monkey or a parrot? Surely not; that would be carrying a surplus to Peru where there were already plenty of monkeys and parrots. How about a pet rat? Bouguer would not bring along such a pet. There were a surplus of those on the *Portefaix*.

I gave up on the subject, and it was only at the end of my stay in Paris that I read, in another description of the Expedition, that it was a savage dog (of whatever kind) that bit Jussieu and, oddly, he was angry not because of the attack, but because Bouguer insisted on disposing of the dog as a dangerous animal.

The privileges of rank were undoubtedly observed on the *Portefaix*, where the scientists were the only passengers, with the best cabins assigned to the three Academy members, the rest making out in second-class quarters. Whatever the cabins occupied, we can be sure that all the Expedition members had a rugged trip. In those days voyages across the Atlantic were always rugged. This was taken for granted and was seldom referred to after the long ordeal was over. Only occasionally some traveler of the early time of transoceanic voyages took the trouble to describe the trip. One early traveler, Eugenio de Salazar, made an Atlantic crossing with his family in 1572 on the *Nuestra Señora de los Remedios*. He wrote it up and it was published in his collected *Letters*.

Starting out with the usual seasickness:

> There we lay . . . white as ghosts, without seeing the sun or the moon; we never opened our eyes, or changed our clothes, or moved, until the third day.
>
> [Then] I dressed as well as I could, and crawled out of the closet in which we lay. I discovered that we were riding on what some people call a wooden horse, or a timber nag, or a flying pig, though to me it looked more like a town. The ship has one or two fountains called pumps, the water from which is unfit for tongue and

palate to taste, or nostrils to smell, or even eyes to see, for it comes out bubbling like Hell and stinking like the Devil. . . . There are very singular pearl-enormous lice, so big that sometimes they are seasick. . . . For game in the neighborhood, there are fine flights of cockroaches . . . and very good rat hunting, the rats so fierce . . . they turn on the hunters like wild boars.

The galley, "pot island" as they call it, is a great scene of bustle and activity at meal times. [The diners] all talk about other food. One will say, "Oh for a bunch of . . . grapes," someone else, "For me, a lettuce and an artichoke head." The worst longing is for something to drink; you are in the middle of the sea, surrounded by water, but they dole out the water for drinking by ounces . . . and all the time you are dying of thirst from eating dried beef and food pickled in brine. . . . Even the water, when you can get it, is so foul that you have to close your eyes and hold your nose before you can drink it.

The situation had not changed much by 1735. The only way to preserve food was by drying or salting, and water stowed in a ship's tanks for weeks turned foul. It would be twenty years before a cure for scurvy was found. Our scientists, however, must have been healthy young men, for no illness is noted. They must have worn the same clothes for days at a time. Those twenty-eight extra suits were probably kept for civilized life ashore. To be sure, the *Portefaix* was not like the *Nuestra Señora de los Remedios* of a century and a half before. It was a naval frigate, built for speed, armed, with gangs of sailors to keep things more or less shipshape.

But thirty-seven days is a long time at sea. And it could have been more. Landfalls were still not accurate. John Harrison in Yorkshire had just completed the first of his five designs for a marine chronometer.

But that is getting ahead of the story. I can imagine the scientists just now assembling on the wharf in La Rochelle. This ancient port dated back centuries before the French scientists gathered there. Two massive fourteenth-century towers with crenelated walls defended the harbor entrance where traffic was heavy. In the eighteenth century, it was a convenient port of arrival or departure for ships crossing the Atlantic along a sea-lane midway between that of England to the north and Spain to the south. There must have been the usual activity of such a port, with ships docking and departing, many of them far less trim and well maintained than the naval frigate *Portefaix*. As they climbed aboard, the scientists must have been glad that the moment of sailing had finally arrived. The screams of seagulls, the shouts of stevedores, the odor of dead fish and mudflats, and the damp fog seeping in through the twin towers at the harbor entrance— all spoke of travel across an ocean to another world.

None of the journals gives details of the voyage from La Rochelle to Martinique in the West Indies, but one can imagine the scientists passing the time with difficulty as they eagerly waited to start their mission. No doubt they were out on deck when the weather was fair, taking sights with their quarts de cercle, watching for flying fish, known as "sea swallows," noting the gradual passage of the constellations across the night sky.

On June 22 the island of Martinique hove in view. The scientists were surely all on deck, surveying the land, by turns, through their two telescopes, checking their compasses and their watches with the up-to-date second hands, perhaps starting the first jottings in their notebooks. They had arrived safely at the other side of the world, four thousand miles from France.

FIVE

WHAT THE FRENCHMEN SAW as they made landfall at Martinique after their long journey was a smallish island, about
fifty miles long and twenty-two wide, rising abruptly from
the sea and divided into three mountainous areas with
Mount Pelée, the famous volcano, jutting up on the right.
They headed inshore for Fort-Royal, the capital city. A brisk
breeze, the constant trade wind, carried them into the
harbor on a starboard tack and they dropped anchor a little
way offshore. No doubt the scientists, who were at such a
time tourists as well, went eagerly in the shore boats to the
wharf.

Jussieu, the botanist, must have been particularly interested in the unfamiliar scene of dense mangrove swamps
and luxurious tropical vegetation. Morning glories and sea
grapes decked the shore, along with ferns and orchids
hanging from trees of unfamiliar species. Above them, further up the mountains, rose stands of lofty mahogany trees,
while the tops of the peaks were bare.

The town was prosperous and the travelers must have feasted, after their weeks of shipboard diet, on the bananas and pineapples and the fine Arabian coffee that was the island's specialty. The inhabitants of Martinique, large numbers of black slaves imported by the Compagnie du Senegal, some surviving Carib Indians, and the ruling class of French traders, were a different population mix from anything at home. The group went sight-seeing and some of them climbed Mount Pelée, where, La Condamine wrote, they "ascended the last part of the way on all fours." When they reached the top, they were immediately greeted by an earthquake.

At Martinique La Condamine fell ill, apparently with yellow fever, known on the island as "fever of Siam." Perhaps . . . but perhaps not, for he adds, "I was sick, I was bled, I was purged and cured and back on board, all in the course of twenty-four hours"—a very quick cure for a serious ailment.

In a few days the group went on to Santo Domingo, presumably on naval business concerning the *Portefaix*. It was a larger port than that in Martinique, well equipped to supply the needs of the Expedition.

They had brought from France one very big comfortable tent with a marquee. They now had two copies made of it so that there was one for each of the Academy members, Godin, Bouguer, and La Condamine. The other scientists were expected to crowd into smaller tents, "cannonières," and perhaps ponder on how soon they could become Academy members and loll in luxury.

Now the group looked about to enlist retainers for the Expedition, but among the white inhabitants of Santo Domingo, there were no takers. They preferred the tropical ease and comforts of their island to travel among rugged mountains in strange unfriendly places. The scientists knew it would be a hard climb up from the ocean to the city of Quito and they must have assistance. They had to make do with slaves who had no choice in the matter. There would be a dozen masters and fourteen servants.

Now they would head, still aboard the *Portefaix*, to Cartagena de las Indias, there to rendezvous with the two Spanish officers, Jorge Juan Santacilla and Antonio de Ulloa.

❦

So far I had followed them close behind, though unobserved, imagining details I did not find described, occasionally interpolating facts that I believed were very likely true. Every morning I went to the Academy, where I delved through letters, notes, and reports. I came away each noon with a small treasure trove of information.

Leaving the scientists en route for Cartagena, I turned my attention to the two young Spaniards who were to meet them there. Their journals were in the library rather than the archives, so for a while I sat there in the mornings, reading but also looking around the grand room, with its eighteenth-century portraits and furniture, reminding myself that this was where the Académie des Sciences met when they planned the "greatest expedition the world had ever seen."

The Spaniards were younger than the Academy members, in their early twenties, but they had graduated with high distinction from officers' school. Jorge Juan was so talented at mathematics that he was nicknamed Euclid. He was fitted out with a fine title for his meeting with the Frenchmen: "Commander of Aliaga in the Order of Mata and Commander of the Marine Guard of Gentlemen." Antonio was named lieutenant in the same company. Officially, they would join in experiments or lend a hand where needed. Unofficially, they would watch those sly Frenchmen to report any attempt they might make to turn from scientists into businessmen, robbing His Majesty of some of the wealth of the New World. Besides this, they had an even more secret mission: to survey Spain's holdings in Peru and report on the behavior of the clergy and the local governments. No doubt there had been complaints. They did so, and their report was so shocking and listed so many evidences of corruption and cruelty that it was not made public for many years. Finally, in 1826, it appeared in a thick volume titled *Noticias Secretas de América* and led to many reforms.

They set out on the sixty-four gun ship *Conqueror* from Cadiz on May 26, 1735, and reached Cartagena Bay on July 9 without stopping anywhere in the West Indies. They waited there for the Frenchmen, who did not arrive for some time, since the *Portefaix* had business in the islands.

Cartagena de las Indias must have reminded the young men of Europe. It was prosperous and very Spanish, with its ornate sixteenth-century cathedral, the main plaza, and the Palace of the Inquisition. It was a busy port, taking on cargo from the cities of South America to send to Spain, and receiving shiploads of slaves.

While they waited for the Frenchmen, Jorge Juan and Antonio made their observations on the social scene in this Latin American port, the first they had visited. The women of Cartagena, Jorge Juan tells us in his journal, were not active. "In the home their whole exercise consists in sitting in their hammocks and swinging themselves for air." However, "both sexes are possessed of a great deal of wit and penetration; and also of a genius in all kinds of mechanic arts. A child of two or three years of age converses with a regularity and seriousness that is rarely seen in Europe at six or seven."

Jorge Juan was a good reporter, noting all sorts of unfamiliar customs. When someone died and became an "angelito," for instance, the corpse was set up in the living room in an open upright coffin. It was made up to be lifelike, with a crown of roses. Cheerful tunes were played and sung.

He had a lively interest in food and wrote down elaborate recipes. Puchero, which he describes as the national dish of Peru, contains beef, pork, smoked mutton, cabbages, sweet potatoes, sausage meat, pigs' feet, yucas, sweet corn, bananas, quinces, and chickpeas. This elaborate mix is heavily salted and cooked over a slow fire for four or five hours.

He noted that chirimoya flowers were used to perfume wardrobes, and that guests brought their own snuff boxes to parties. "The guest took out his snuff box or extracted a pinch of snuff from it, blowing on it to eliminate the dust, then inhaled deeply, even if he sneezed."

This was just the man to bring back news, both good and bad, of social life in King Philip's realms in the New World.

I had now been two weeks in Paris. The canicule had moderated and I noted fewer desperate measures. Men no longer walked along the Quais in swimming shorts, and women went back to their stylish, well-fitted dresses from the loose smocks they had dug out of the attic for the heat wave.

It was almost the end of July, and promptly on August 1 Paris would experience its annual hegira from the hot pavements to the crowded beaches. The archives would be open until the middle of the month, giving me time to finish reading. I was used to the city now and to my small hotel where, now that the canicule was over, my room was comfortable enough. With habit taking over, as it does even in strange places, I now had my special bench by the water where, looking along the Seine to the left, I could see the glittering gold of the statues on the Pont Alexandre III, newly refurbished to stand out against the gray sky. Across the river, tenants came and went from time to time to the houseboats tied up along the shore. It would be pleasant to live in one, with a flower garden in the cockpit and the gentle surge of the river gliding by. The rent, I reminded myself, would be fantastic.

In the other direction I could see as far as the Ile de la Cité and Notre Dame, hazy in the river mist. On the left bank a smart sailing yacht was tied up, sails neatly furled, hatches closed, no one aboard. I wondered several times who the owners might be.

I enjoyed staying in my small hotel in the Seventh Arrondissement, a section on the Left Bank between the ancient university quarter and Napoleon's tomb in the Invalides. I couldn't have chosen a better neighborhood in which to savor reminders of the eighteenth-century city: the Palais-Bourbon, with a view of the Place de la Concorde just across the river, and the magnificent residences of the Boulevard Saint-Germain. I don't know where Monsieur de La Condamine lived in Paris, but I like to think it was here.

Isabel Godin kept no journal or, if she did, it has not come down to us. Yet her memory today is at least as fresh as that of any scientist of the group. I pass my mornings in the Academy archives looking up details of the French Expedition, but I also spend time during these weeks in Paris thinking about the "first woman to go down the Amazon." There are satisfying details in Jean Godin's letter to La Condamine describing her desperate wanderings. It adds to my interest to know exact details, even small ones: the three spotted birds' eggs she found, perhaps those of a partridge, and her difficulty in swallowing them because starvation had constricted her throat; the throbbing pain from a thorn that had embedded itself in the base of her thumb. I am interested to learn that she valued material things: the three skirts of velvet, taffeta, and satin, the favorite emerald-studded earrings.

Much is still missing. I want to know more than the facts, no matter how fascinating. I have developed a personal bond with this woman. If I had been born two centuries earlier or she in modern times, we would have had much to say to each other. I want to know what she felt, not only wandering by herself in the wilds, but during the rest of her long journey.

In his description of her days in the jungle, Jean Godin tells us merely, "The remembrance of the shocking spectacle she witnessed, the horror incident on her solitude and the darkness of night, . . . the perpetual apprehension of death . . . had such effect on her spirits as to cause her hair to turn gray."

One day I sought the house where as a student I had spent the winter. It was on the Ile de Saint-Louis, an island in the middle of the river, and its facade overlooked the Seine. The building was a palace of the grandest sort, six stories tall, with an enormous inner courtyard and four flights of stone stairs at the corners leading upward all the way to the attic. The attic was where my friend Frances and I lived, crouching over the fireplace in the winter when the Seine far below our windows froze solid. Small comfort in the cold that the back of the hearth showed the date 1498, or that this palace had been the home of Louis XIV's finance minister. The attic rooms had a rent we could afford, fifteen dollars a month, if I remember correctly. We shared a toilet with some fishermen and their families, who provided us with fresh caught fish and laughed at our foreign ways. Now, I would like to have gone inside again and climbed those stairs worn down by centuries of footsteps, but there was a uniformed guard on the door, and no entrance. This has become one of the most select addresses in all Paris.

I described my project to the young man who ran my hotel. He was surprised that a tourist, member of a transient breed, should stay a whole month in his Hôtel du Palais-Bourbon, attractive though it no doubt was. He listened patiently as I described my project then turned back eagerly to his favorite modern toys—the fax, the telex, and the computer. His elderly mother, who really ran the hotel, seized on my reference to Saint-Amand Montrond.

"In the Berry, n'est-ce pas? I had an uncle there. When I was a child I visited, but it has been too many years. I will write and ask him about the family."

She had not heard when I left Paris, but I have no doubt she would have found a link, however weak, with my eighteenth-century characters.

I became interested in local French matters and eagerly scanned *Le Figaro*, which arrived each morning with my petit déjeuner. They had a splendid series about memories of World War II, but I would miss the liberation of Paris when I left for home on August 15. My time in France was limited. I must get on with my reading.

The Spaniards waited in Cartagena for the Frenchmen for some weeks. When they arrived they would all set out together on the next leg of the voyage, from Cartagena to Portobelo. Looking at the map, it seemed to me that these travelers were taking the long way around: Martinique to Santo Domingo, down to Cartagena on the northwest coast of South America, then across to Portobelo on the Atlantic side of the Panama peninsula. From there they would have to follow an overland track, using carts and mules and slaves, to Panama City. Thence, they would proceed by ship down the west coast of South America to Guayaquil, the port for northern Peru, from which they could climb up to Quito.

Why not go overland directly from Cartagena south to Quito, covering the eight hundred miles through the mountains to their destination? At least they would be on dry land. They decided, however, that their baggage was too heavy and too fragile for such a route, even though the annual gold trains managed it. Reading about this route, I could see why sea voyages, however circuitous, would be preferable.

At the end of the eighteenth century, the route was still tremendously difficult. It took the explorer Humboldt and his friend Bonpland four months for the journey from Bogotá to Quito, along a way so narrow that mules were sometimes unable to follow its precipitous windings. When travelers from opposite directions met, one party had to retreat or else climb up the cliff, hanging by roots or outcroppings until the others had passed beneath them.

On November 24 the whole party embarked on board a French frigate—not the *Portefaix*—for Portobelo, where they arrived on the twenty-ninth. It rained constantly while they were in this port, and they observed that the inhabitants combated the somber climate by drinking a glass of brandy every morning at eleven o'clock. Since, as Jorge Juan noted in his journal, they also bathed every day at eleven, it made for a crowded schedule. The scientists remarked on the presence of thousands of toads in the streets. From the surrounding forest came the "horrible cries" of the sloth, known sarcastically as "Perico Liger" or "Nimble Peter" for his painfully slow progress from branch to branch. At night bats hovered above the streets in clouds.

In the time of the yearly galleonfair Portobelo was the center for all commerce between Europe and the southern sea. The town was known as the "Tomb of Spaniards" since a third or more of the crews of visiting ships died of illness brought on by the continual rain. The Expedition members escaped fatal illness, but La Condamine was stung by a scorpion and they all suffered mysterious fevers from time to time.

They were glad to leave Portobelo and proceed overland to Panama, where La Condamine made a chart of the bay. He also observed with fascination not only the attractions of the women, but their peculiar habits, especially their manner of smoking: "They roll the tobacco into slender rolls and put the lighted part of the roll into their mouths and there continue it a long time without its being quenched, or the fire incommoding them."

Finally the party took ship down the west coast of South America to the port of Manta, halfway between the equator and Guayaquil. They crossed the equatorial line on March 7–8 and reached Manta on March 19, 1736.

They had been almost a year on the journey, but time was different then. It stretched to amazing lengths; months turned into years, years into decades. Yet men had short life spans. They would have to exert themselves to the utmost to accomplish their ambitions within the time fate allotted.

SIX

Paris, July–August, 1991

IN THE EVENINGS IN Paris I sorted through my notes. This to me is the hardest part of research. Evidently I have not the scholarly mind. Cards become jumbled, handwriting illegible even though it's my own and I understood it when I wrote it down. The archive files were not helpful since the contents were arranged haphazardly: a dinner party where La Condamine gave a learned speech in his old age could be side by side with jottings for the journal he was just starting twenty years before.

However, I was beginning to know the characters in the story. The solemn scientists at the equator were turning into young men with different, sometimes antagonistic, characters. Some details were emerging from the chaos.

Pierre Bouguer noted that the corn biscuits in the camping supplies were "too dry." He complained that "we had to work in places where the only trails were those of wild animals." He spoke of the "repugnance my weak health had given me for sea voyages." However, his ailments did not prevent his work on a multitude of projects outlined in his journal: "to correct the maps of the countries through which we had to pass; to make observations on the loadstone, examine the weight of the air, its degree of condensation, elasticity, refraction and many other things, as occasion would offer." He was already known for a variety of scholarly findings: the apparent brightness of celestial objects compared to that of a candle flame, the horizontal gravitational pull of mountains, the absorption of light in the atmosphere.

All surviving portraits of the scientists show them cut from one mold, that of the busts at the equator, fixed permanently in middle age, overweight, with the solemnity of the lecture platform. I gradually separated these men in my mind's eye. Bouguer has the look of a hypochondriac who, however, will work as hard as anyone while at the same time letting the world know that it's not easy. Eventually he developed gout, although, as La Condamine remarked unsympathetically, "he drank milk not wine." At thirty-eight, he was one of the oldest of the scientists, beyond the age of adventurous mountain climbing. (Still, he did get where they were all going.) One hopes that his sensational observations were worth the hardships of the trip. There was the evening when he saw two suns setting because of "astronomic refractions," and another occasion when from Pambamarca Volcano he observed "triple circular iris arches formed by the light of the moon."

Perhaps it is because of what I know of his behavior that Louis Godin looks somewhat frivolous. His eyes seem to rove a bit towards a desirable object. However, the viewer can bring all sorts of wrong interpretations to something seen, and Louis Godin's severe bust at the equator may have portrayed the whole man. But I have doubts. Perhaps freedom from a humdrum domestic life attracted him to the Expedition. He was the only married member, leaving a wife and two children at home in France. He was a revered astronomer. The English had invited him to London to choose the lenses for his instruments and he spent three months there.

However, scientific projects could not always compete with other attractions. When the party was held over in Santo Domingo waiting for transportation to Cartagena, he fell for the charms of a local girl, described as an "avid beauty." Her tastes were extravagant. I can imagine Louis Godin escorting her around the town, buying meals at expensive restaurants, spending moonlit evenings at the beach, hanging about in shops while dresses and jewelry were selected, ignoring the criticism of the other scientists who saw this liaison doing harm to their plans.

Jean Godin, Louis's twenty-one-year-old cousin, made no mention of Louis's conduct in any records that have come down to us, but then I imagine young Jean as an inexperienced, perhaps naive, fellow who had come along for the adventure, very far in appearance and personality from the stodgy bust erected in his memory at the equator. He was not a born scholar and probably not a bon vivant either. If he makes no mention of his older cousin's escapades, that does not mean that he approved of them. During most of the years in Peru he was closer to La Condamine, helping him in his experiments, planning to follow him down the Amazon. Jean's memory is associated especially with that of Isabel, his wife, and the history of their devotion.

I reminded myself that there really is no chance of understanding people of another country who have been gone for two hundred years. However, an irresistible urge leads me to imagine and recreate them. Of all the scientists,

La Condamine had the most individuality. I can distinctly see him as a young man of "burning ambition," keen on getting ahead no matter who might be in the way, then as an explorer, fascinated by every unfamiliar detail in the scene around him, and finally as a testy old man with an ear trumpet, boring his colleagues at the Academy with endless reminiscences.

Most interesting to me is Isabel Godin, and she is the hardest to visualize. Was she simply the victim of circumstances, a high-class, eighteenth-century lady cast into a horrific adventure? Or was she more special than that? Did she seek adventure, although not, certainly, the ultimate disaster? I need more information.

※

When the party reached Manta, Bouguer and La Condamine went ashore, leaving the others to go on to Guyaquil by ship. At Manta, the two observed the equinox, located the point where the equator reached the ocean, and saw an eclipse of the moon. They recorded their stay on a rock at Palmar, where the inscription can still be seen. Then they set out inland, drawing a map of the territory as they went.

Meanwhile, Jorge Juan, Godin, Jussieu, and the rest of the Expedition members proceeded by ship to Guayaquil from where they took the usual overland route to Quito. It was a series of trails climbing from sea level forty leagues up to an altitude of twelve thousand feet, with higher elevations on some parts of the way. It was a journey of more than two months. They had exchanged the slaves for Indian bearers and they set out on the trek heavily laden.

Jorge Juan describes the journey in detail. From the beginning, he tells us, the climb was tremendously difficult, through uninhabited territory of ravines, swamps, rivers. The travelers suffered frequent falls and bruises, but rejoiced that they had no serious accidents. Jorge Juan wrote in his journal, describing "abysses which made us shudder with fear . . . passages where the bravest could not walk without trembling in terror . . . particularly if one considered the proximity of the danger and the little distance it was from the animals to whom were consigned something as precious as life, and the precipices which seemed to be there to engulf us."

The mules could only proceed if little trenches were dug across the road to keep them from sliding down in the mud. They plodded along trembling and snorting, sometimes sinking so far into the ditches that they drew their bellies and the riders' legs along the ground. I had seen an engraving of this scene as a chapter heading in Jorge Juan's journal.

When they finally reached the town of Chimbo high up in the mountains, the travelers were surprised to hear all the bells in the place ringing and every house resounding with the blare of trumpets, tabors, and pipes. A fiesta? No, the townsfolk always put on a show to congratulate anyone who came that way. It was hard to believe that by this route Riobamba and Quito imported wine, salt, cotton, fish, oil. They could only do this in the summer. In the winter no mules could make it, and that was called the "closing of the mountain."

La Condamine and Bouguer, taking the route from Manta inland, also had adventures, which La Condamine recorded in his journal: storms, robbers, lost baggage when one of the pack mules stumbled into a gully. Snakes appeared in the shacks where they camped; weevils munched on their provisions; stingless bees settled on the horses to suck up their sweat; army ants eagerly chewed on everything. At night, the travelers battled swarms of voracious mosquitoes and flying cockroaches "the size of mice."

The whole terrain was covered with thick woods where they had to use hatchets to get through, and they went more often on foot than on horseback. It rained every afternoon. They lugged much heavy equipment, including a quart de cercle that two Indians could hardly carry. They crossed torrential streams on lianas stretched over the water like fishnets. They ran out of powder and provisions and spent eight days in wild country abandoned by their guides. Fever struck them and they had nothing to eat but bananas and other wild fruits.

However, this was adventure and there were good things. La Condamine saw the emerald mines on the river Bichile, and heard the story of an emerald the size of an ostrich egg to which an Indian temple had been dedicated. He carried always his compass and his thermometer to record various findings, and he collected interesting plants all along the route. On the way he discovered that rubber would stretch, and made a sheet of it to protect his octant from the incessant rains. At night, Bouguer watched the transit of Venus through his telescope while La Condamine wrote down his day's observations. On the few nights when there was no rain, the moon shone with tropical brilliance and the Southern Cross was clearly visible. Locusts and tiny frogs whirred and croaked in the darkness. Branches rustled and cracked as some animal moved through them. The scent of strange flowers hung heavy in the sultry air.

Part way on the journey La Condamine met a young man, Pedro Vicente Maldonado from the town of Riobamba, who had hurried to find and join the scientist. Bouguer had always disapproved of La Condamine's character, especially his "licentiousness" (of which no details are given). After a couple of weeks of traveling with him, he was glad to leave, taking the heavy baggage with him while La Condamine went on with his new friend.

This left the two men to travel at leisure, Maldonado introducing the Frenchman to the wonders of the new country. They went by dugout up the Esmeralda River to the Rio Verde and up that river to meet the Cayapes Indians, with La Condamine busy along the way, mapping the country and noting unfamiliar trees, plants, birds, monkeys, and frogs. He took samples of a strange metal from the riverbank and named it "platinum." He met the friendly Colorado Indians, who were dressed entirely in stripes of red paint. In their enthusiasm for their new friend, the Indians embraced La Condamine, leaving his coat and stockings covered with bright scarlet dye.

❧

On my first visit to South America some years ago, I made a side trip from Quito to find and photograph the Colorado Indians.

It was a chilly morning, the volcanoes standing up in frigid splendor around the high valley.

"The bus ride will be interesting," the hotel manager told me, "and I hope you find the Colorados."

Pulling my sweater around me, I walked to the bus station and climbed aboard the bus marked "Santo Domingo de los Colorados." All sorts of passengers were starting the journey, families with unwieldy baskets and jugs of something to drink, a teenage football team, a priest, several old women and young men. No Colorados on the bus, but I understood that they never left their town of Santo Domingo to come to the city. Why should they? A couple of irate hens tied by the feet to the overhead rack noisily completed the passenger list.

We set out, climbed over the ridge surrounding the city, and started down . . . down. The driver was evidently late for an important engagement in Santo Domingo. We barreled at breakneck speed around curves and across rickety bridges. Stands of trees, a river, little villages, we galloped through them all, leaving me hardly enough time to note the change from alpine scenery to lowlands to tropical marshes and coconut palms with vines throttling trees along the way. I was more or less following La Condamine's journey except that he was going up, not down, by slow mule, not bus, through strange country. I was taking a comfortable journey of a few hours to a familiar destination—to the bus driver anyway. La Condamine spent many weeks on the way.

I wish I could say that at Santo Domingo I immediately found myself among throngs of friendly red-painted Indians, but that was not the case. No Indians of any kind were in sight. Just a rather scruffy market specializing in tired cabbages and onions, cheap tennis shoes, and tiny dried shrimp. Dilapidated houses lined the main street. It began to rain. I had coffee in a two-table cafe and wondered what to do next. The taxi driver who was resting at the other table, his cab parked conveniently in front, leaned my way.

"Where would you like to go, Señorita?"

What I thought was, home, that's where I want to go. Instead I said, "Can you take me to see the Colorado Indians?"

"The Colorados?" The man hesitated. "They don't come here to the market. Pues, tal vez . . . I could take you to see the chief. Good friend of mine. He lives in a big house, always happy to see visitors."

I pictured the chief, who had surely changed his stripes for jeans or tennis shorts, greeting me politely and offering me a beer in his comfortable condo.

"No thank you," I told the cab driver. "It's getting late. I must go back to Quito."

Later I heard that the Indians did live outside of town, were still painted, and probably awaited photographers. Would they have embraced me as they had La Condamine?

At Puerto de Quito the trail left the river for the three-day climb to the capital. The Colorados stayed around, leading the travelers up Nono Volcano to a high point at twelve thousand feet. La Condamine now found that his stockings and coat were torn and ruined. He changed into woolen trousers and a poncho.

As he neared Quito he entered a new world of bare cliffs, icy summits, snowcapped volcanoes, and high plains. Strange-looking llamas wandered in herds on the upland meadows. The dense trees of lowland forests were replaced by scrawny wind-twisted bushes, by alpine flowers, red and purple geraniums, and the ichu grass on which the llamas grazed. Condors soared majestically overhead, their huge wings motionless. From their white summits some of the volcanoes belched black smoke that dissipated like streamers in the pale blue sky. La Condamine felt the oppression of soroche, the mountain sickness. Now he and his companion had become friends and Maldonado had unofficially joined the Expedition.

The inhabitants of Quito, meanwhile, eagerly awaited the arrival of this group of important European scientists. Under seal of 14 August, 1734, King Philip V had sent word to the viceroys, the presidents of the audiencias, and the governors in America that "they should offer every assistance to the expedition, including taking from the royal treasury any money necessary to maintain them."

On May 29 all the members of the French Geodesic Mission came together in the city, almost exactly twelve months since they had set sail from France. They found the place strange and exciting, a pocket of civilization in the highland, which they had reached after weeks of hardship in wild country.

The city found its visitors even more exciting. Dignitaries assembled, important visitors rode in from surrounding towns, the president of the audiencia, the clergy, all distinguished persons formed a welcoming committee. The honored guests would be put up for the first three days in the municipal palace on the main square, then moved to comfortable lodgings.

To the citizens of Quito, far from their roots in Europe, the arrival of the Frenchmen was a unique opportunity for a grand parade. Drums beat, bells tolled, Indians danced to the plaintive music of flutes while native children in brilliant blue tunics marched behind their Dominican teachers who waved banners of bright colors. Solemn speeches were delivered, welcoming the learned visitors, the "measurers of the arc." Very likely nobody in town was qualified to understand what "measuring the arc" might be, or the years of work it would entail, but this was the most important local event of the century. It rivaled in excitement the day, two centuries before, when the first white women arrived in Quito.

No doubt the Frenchmen made the most of such a fine welcome, changing into fresh suits, donning their dress swords, dusting their wigs with powder, and breaking open the barrels of good French brandy.

Only La Condamine was very much miffed because he had nothing suitable to wear. The Colorados had smeared his clothes with red paint, and what hadn't been smeared had been torn climbing jagged peaks. The woolen trousers and poncho in which he ended his journey were clothes he considered unworthy of Quito society. The contingent coming up from Guayaquil brought sixty-six mule loads of baggage, but his spare suits were not among them. He spent several days incognito until his gear arrived, hiding in the Jesuit convent from which he went out only one evening, disguised in a borrowed cloak, to call upon the city president, returning to the convent in the dark.

Jorge Juan continued his journal, describing the life of this exotic city. Every detail was of interest. He noted that the city dwellers, who often had country haciendas as well, loved gambling, dancing the fandango, and drinking eau-de-vie or the native liquor, chicha, which he judged undrinkable. The ice for their drinks was fetched from Pichincha Volcano. Even the moderately well-off ate from silver dishes.

There seemed to be more women than men in Quito, Jorge Juan observed, concluding that women were stronger than men. Society consisted of Spaniards of pure blood, then the mixed-race cholos, and below them in social standing black slaves imported from the West Indies and the picturesque native Indians who "seem to think their hair part of themselves" (an odd, unexplained remark) and who made merry with dances, wearing ribbon masks. The Spanish gentlemen sported black capes, short tight knee breeches, silk stockings, and dress swords. The cholos appeared in "Quito blue cloth" with a ribbon belt and a sort of turban. Indians dressed in ankle-length white cotton pants and long white shirts.

Young Couplet, the teenage boy in the party, wrote home telling his mother how the New World ladies dressed and did their hair:

"Every part of the women's dresses of Quito is covered with lace. . . . They arrange their hair in braids with which they form a sort of cross at the base of the neck; they put a ribbon on their heads, called a balaca, with which they make some turns around their hair, making with the ends of this a sort of rose shape on their foreheads. These women are enchanting . . ."

Couplet, along with the other young foreigners, must have enjoyed to the full the company of these pretty, unsophisticated girls, teaching them the latest dance steps from Paris, giving news (the first news they had ever had) of French fashions, and sharing the secrets of French cooking with their mothers. Everything French became the rage. New gowns were run up, rare French wines were brought out of the cellars, and the gossip of French salons was passed around, although it was by now a year old and nobody understood it anyway.

Perhaps it was at this time that Isabel Grandmaison, one of the principal characters in this story, first met the Frenchmen. Her father, General Grandmaison, was one of those "distinguished persons" who very likely came to greet the visiting scientists from his hacienda in Riobamba, south of Quito. He may have brought his favorite daughter to the capital with him, although in 1736 she was only eight years old. She was precocious, speaking French and Spanish, playing music, painting pictures. She was notably pretty—La Condamine, a connoisseur in such matters, referred to her as "delicious" with a "provocative mouth"—and curious to know what the world was like outside her small territory in Peru. Perhaps she started then to think of the excitement of travel, and of faraway Paris, unaware of the dreadful journey she would someday undertake.

The scientists, after a year of travel and anticipation, were now ready at last to start their official labors.

⚜

I considered taking the train south to Saint-Amand Montrond where Isabel and Jean Godin had lived. There could be a wealth of material there. However, it was a three-hour journey from Paris, and the canicule, which had returned, discouraged me from strenuous effort. Remembering my lack of success in Riobamba, I could easily imagine arriving in Saint-Amand Montrond, going to the tourist office, the cultural center, or the library, inquiring after Jean and Isabel Godin:

"Who? When were they here? Our records go back many years, of course."

"They lived here two hundred and fifty years ago."

"Ah well, Mademoiselle, after all . . . Quel dommage. We have no records. Time and also the Revolution, not to mention the two world wars. What a shame that you came all the way from Paris."

In Paris I had come to the end of my time. I looked with satisfaction at my bundle of notes and went one last time to the archives to say goodbye and thanks. As a rule, the files contained material about Academy members only, not lesser scientists. However, on the off chance, I inquired whether there was anything under the name of Jean Godin, Louis Godin's cousin. A slender folder was handed to me, and in it, to my excitement, I discovered that the past had found its way down through time to the present! Here was the text of a lecture given in 1989 by Isabel Godin's great-great-great-great-great-great-nephew, Monsieur Marc Lemaire, on the subject of his aunt's life and adventures. Making this leap through history, I had a photocopy run off to take home with me. I now had the feeling that progress was at last being made in my research, and at the same time I realized that getting to know Isabel meant a great deal more to me than my usual writing contacts. Perhaps now I would feel that I knew someone I was writing about even through the fog of two hundred years.

Someone had scribbled Monsieur Lemaire's address at the bottom of the speech. Marly-le-roi. Not far from Paris. I tried to call Monsieur Lemaire but got no answer. He must have fled the city in the August exodus. I would write to him later. Meantime, the speech showed me that Isabel was far from forgotten. I wished I had taken the train to Saint-Amand.

On my last day in Paris, as I rode along the Boulevard Saint-Germain on a bus, I thought of La Condamine taking this same route when the rows of massive six-story mansions housed the social elite. Now they were divided into apartments, doctors' offices, restaurants, and cafes. Traffic sped by and on the sidewalks pedestrians hurried to the metro entrance. Still, I could imagine La Condamine in his later years, his notes and ear trumpet in hand, bowling down the boulevard in his chaise, intent on arriving in good time at the weekly session of the Academy. There were always fresh details to tell them of those long-ago adventures in Peru.

SEVEN

Mexico, Fall 1991–Winter 1992

AT HOME IN MEXICO I sorted my notes according to historical events, the Expedition's findings, the experiences of the scientists as recorded in their journals. I kept a separate list of curious details that struck my fancy:

Bouguer saw an earthworm longer than his arm and thicker than his thumb.

Howling monkeys are about the size of a common terrier and clad in long, soft, maroon-colored hair.

Incidentally, monkey soup is quite tasty.

The toucan was called "predicador," or preacher, because of its propensity for constant exhortation.

The vampire bat is two feet long with its wings extended; its nostrils are fitted as a suction apparatus.

Tapirs are as large as bullocks and taste like beef.

A gang of red monkeys makes a noise like the grunting of a herd of enraged hogs.

These pieces of incidental information do not fit into the

overall picture, I suppose, but I am glad to know them. If for nothing else, they would be useful in a game of "Jeopardy."

In the eighteenth century, South America was still a mysterious continent, especially the vast territory of Peru on the Pacific coast. The monsters of myth were hardly exorcised. Much was rumor, as though a dense fog hung over the land. The secrecy of the Spanish government made the fog thicker. One big contribution made by the members of the French Expedition was to clear away the mist and bring back factual reports. Jorge Juan and Antonio added to this with their detailed sociological notes on corruption and cruelty as they found it in the Spanish realms of the New World.

Meanwhile the scientists were busy, each in his own field. Jussieu collected and classified plants. Louis Godin and Bouguer observed the stars from the frozen summits of Pichincha, Cotopaxi, Sangay, with young Jean Godin along to help build shelters, hold surveying chains, and jot down notes. Hugot, the watchmaker, tinkered with instruments that got out of order. Dr. Seniergues stood by to help with medical advice and treatment. La Condamine spread his talents in all directions, taking sights, drawing maps, making mathematical deductions, collecting plant specimens.

In the pleasant social atmosphere of Quito the Frenchmen recovered quickly from their arduous journey, all except the boy Couplet. La Condamine had the sad task of notifying the boy's uncle, the treasurer of the Academy: "Of my companions of the voyage, Monsieur Couplet, the most robust and one of the youngest, was carried off, three days after his arrival, by a putrid fever."

The central project of the Mission was to measure the distances between the first three degrees of latitude by means of triangulations extending two hundred miles from

Quito to the city of Cuenca. This is still the method used in surveying and civil engineering for measuring precise distances. It is based on the fact that if two angles of a triangle are known, the third can be calculated by methods of plane geometry. By constructing a series of such triangles, values can be obtained for distances not otherwise measurable.

On my two trips to the equator I had noticed that the country around it was rough, with gullies, sharp ridges, hardly a level spot to be found. The scientists searched the cliffs and valleys for a flat place in which to set up an exact baseline, using a six-foot iron bar, a "toise." From this line other accurate measurements could be made. They located two points as centers for their studies, at Carambaro and Oyambaro, close to the equator. La Condamine divided the men into two groups to take independent surveys. Each man had a quart de cercle to measure altitude; with these they made two or three recordings of the same angle, sometimes with different results. From August 1737 to the end of July 1739, one party headed by La Condamine made observations in thirty-five places, the other, headed by Louis Godin, in thirty-two.

Nowadays when travelers set out for faraway destinations they are prepared with all sorts of advance information from guidebooks, maps, descriptions written by former tourists or explorers. Before my first trip to South America I had read about Quito, seen a program on television, studied a map. As we circled over the Quito airport preparing to land, I was impressed but not surprised by the majestic landscape. For the scientists, it must have been different. They had little advance knowledge of what they would find in Peru. Perhaps if they had known more about the volcanoes, they would not have agreed to spend years working in mountains whose summits, as La Condamine wrote, were "lost in the clouds, almost all covered with enormous masses of snow as ancient as the world."

When the five-mile baseline at the equator was completed, the scientists proceeded to measure their two-hundred-mile series of triangles south to Cuenca. This involved signaling to each other from the various volcanoes along the route. Indians kept purloining the signals, which at first were pyramids of three or four long branches of aloe covered with straw or light-colored cotton. When these vanished, the scientists used piles of stones with a cross on top. These disappeared too and finally, at the suggestion of Louis Godin, they took to using their sleeping tents as signals. The lesser members of the Expedition had to transport and set up the large tents for the three Academicians as well as their own small shelters.

Meanwhile other experiments were carried on, each man in his own field. Dilation of metals was observed in the sun, in boiling water, and in snow. La Condamine and Jussieu studied quinine (cinchona), sending samples to the Jardin des Plantes in Paris, along with curupa seeds (ground up to create an inhaled hallucinatory drug), and cochineal insects for dye.

At intervals, boxes were sent off to the Academy, going by muleback to Cartagena, thence by ship to France. A list of one of these shipments shows the diverse interests of the Expedition members. It contained "a silver Inca vase and silver idols of Peru; many ancient crystal vases with animals, some of them whistling; fossil shells; a beautiful marine plant attached to a smooth pebble; seventeen rare shells; a magnet from Guanicabalicca; a molar tooth, petrified in agate, weighing two pounds; various dry and liquid balms; an Inca dictionary and grammar; petrified wood; ancient stone hatchets; a little crocodile from the river of Guayaquil; the head and skin of a coral snake."

One interesting batch failed to arrive. A box containing "monstrous bones of giants" was opened on shipboard and believed by the superstitious sailors to be bad luck. After deliberating and taking signed votes from all the passengers, they threw the whole shipment into the sea. I could find no mention of what these giants were presumed to be.

Along the way, as they climbed among the volcanoes, the scientists found a few rubies and garnets in a river, and discovered mercury mines and rich sources of marble and quartz. They noted these but did not have the opportunity, or for that matter the finances, to develop them. Before the last triangular point had been fixed on the cathedral at Cuenca, the Frenchmen had climbed most of the volcanoes in the area, including Cotopaxi, where flames belched two hundred feet in the air. Their highest point of observation, on Mount Sinauhuan, was so dangerous that in the neighboring villages special prayers were said for the safety of the observers.

The Quiteños were quickly exhausted by their royal welcome for the Frenchmen. Perhaps they felt condescension from the visitors or found their worldly attitude unseemly. Whatever the reason, after only a short time hospitality wore thin. The hosts became suspicious of these strangers, so earnest in their devotion to mysterious scientific activities, so odd in their language and their manners. Never mind that this was the usual behavior of Parisians—who was to know that in the audiencia of Quito?

They observed the foreigners trudging to a deserted spot a few kilometers from Quito, dragging with them their weird instruments: quadrants, telescopes, theodolites, barometers, measuring rods and chains, all of which were apparently enormously valuable and fragile. And for what purpose? No high-class Spaniard would lead such a rugged life. The scientific explanation made no sense. There could be only one answer. There must be money in it somewhere. The newcomers must be after gold. Surely no one would be stupid enough to sail from Europe across half the world and spend miserable months in the icy highlands of the Andes merely to look at the stars and measure the earth's shape. Who cared where the equator went on the earth's surface? It was invisible and that was enough.

The members of the Expedition went doggedly on with their work, measuring the earth, peering at the stars, scaling volcanoes from which they sent mysterious signals to each other. Jorge Juan wrote in his journal: "The serenity in which we live on high mountains swept by wind and hail. . . . The tranquility and constance in which we pass from one scene of desolate solitude to another only feed their suspicions. . . . Some consider us little better than lunatics. Others impute our whole proceedings to the fact that we are endeavoring to discover some rich mineral or buried treasure. . . . When we inform them of the real motive of the expedition it always causes much astonishment."

If the scientists wondered why the citizens of Quito believed them to be treasure hunting, it was because they did not know the history of the country. It would seem an unrealistic dream to expect to discover riches in the miles and miles of rugged gullies, cliffs, and plains around the city, but the suspicions were very well based on stories that had come down from old Inca times.

It was the Incas' misfortune to have enormous supplies of gold and silver when the Spanish conquistadors arrived. To the Incas the metals were beautiful, to be worked into splendid pieces and trimmed with jewels. In Cuzco they even had a golden enclosure, the curicancha, where golden ears of corn appeared to grow, tassels and all, planted in lumps of gold instead of earth. Golden lizards and frogs, butterflies and birds crouched between the plants or perched on golden boughs. Golden grass, golden weeds; among the riches of the curicancha twenty golden llamas and their herdsmen, life-sized in the precious metal.

Yet they did not value gold and silver as a means of barter. It did not represent wealth. They were amazed at the Spaniards' terrible thirst for riches. Did they eat gold?

In November 1532—a full two centuries before the French scientists came to Quito—Francisco Pizarro captured the Inca emperor Atahuallpa in Cajamarca, south of Quito. The Inca had come to a prearranged interview, under a pledge of peace, riding in his solid-gold litter (it weighed a hundred pounds, the Spaniards figured), carried by sixteen bearers. Hundreds of supporters, in checked livery, preceded him to sweep pebbles and sticks out of the way. Many of the Spaniards, it was said, were so frightened that "they could not hold their water."

The Spanish plan worked easily. A friar approached the Inca with peaceful gestures. Then suddenly the Spanish forces launched a terrifying attack, with the raucous music of fifes and drums punctuated by the mysterious roar of gunfire. Pizarro had hardly time to cry "Saint James and at them!" when Atahuallpa fell from his litter, abandoned by his followers who were slaughtered by the thousands. Soon he had exchanged his golden litter for a seat on the floor of a mud hut.

From my acquaintance with early sources, the histories of Cieza de Leon and Garcilaso de la Vega, I knew what happened next. Atahuallpa was, in the best terrorist tradition, put up for ransom. He sounds like a sympathetic human being. He made some friends among the Spaniards, was noted as "always carefully groomed and extremely clean." "He never spat on the ground," the chronicler assures us, "but always in the hand of a woman, out of dignity." He learned chess and became expert at it.

Meantime, the Incas in the enormous realm were gathering the required booty to exchange for their ruler's life. Enough treasure must be delivered to Cajamarca to fill a room twenty by seventeen feet to a height of nine feet. Atahuallpa's loyal subjects accomplished this, sending trains of llamas carrying gold, silver, and jewels for hundreds of miles to meet the Spaniards' demands. However, instead of keeping his word, Pizarro executed the Inca ruler. Natives were still hauling treasure to the city, some of it from Quito. Instantly, as soon as the terrible word of Atahuallpa's death was received, gold and silver statues, golden plates, and jewels were hidden. They were buried in the ground, secreted in lonely caves, tossed into the depths of lakes and rivers. Two hundred years later there was believed still to be an enormous quantity of riches waiting for whomever could find it. Some of it no doubt still waits today.

Modern Ecuador and Peru are still home to millions of indigenous people who speak Quechua, not Spanish. On my trips to South America, I met and talked with some of them, with the help of an interpreter. They seem to be friendly enough to modern civilization but unwilling to be part of it. Folklore and traditions persist. The death of Atahuallpa is still remembered in song:

> *The cruel whites*
> *Who were seeking gold*
> *Invaded us like a plague.*

After capturing our Father Inca,
After gaining his trust,
They gave him death.
With the savagery of the puma,
With the cunning of the fox,
As if he were a llama
They slaughtered him.

The Frenchmen probably did not know the story of Atahuallpa or the reason for the local residents' suspicions. If they had, perhaps they would have done a little prospecting from time to time. Certainly Louis Godin, who liked the high life and was always in debt, would have been tempted. Meantime the Frenchmen were actually very short of funds. Money expected from Paris had not arrived although they had been eighteen months gone. La Condamine opened a boutique in Quito, selling furniture, silk for mantillas, fine handkerchiefs, holland shirts, and a cross of Saint Lazare with diamonds. Where did he get this merchandise? He stated that it was just extra belongings that he happened to have with him. But several of the group went to Cartagena on mysterious errands, probably buying goods for resale. The Spanish authorities complained and La Condamine was soon engaged in the first of many lawsuits. In September 1737, the court in Quito ordered the Geodesic Mission to suspend measurements of the equator, if that was what they were really doing, and not prospecting for gold on Mount Pichincha or importing contraband from the coast.

There was nothing for the Expedition to do but go to Lima, a six-week journey, and beg permission from the viceroy of Peru to continue their work. La Condamine and Jorge Juan made the long trip. It was far from easy. Jorge Juan, in his journal, spoke of the mosquitoes: "At night we suffered insupportable pains. The stings penetrated our clothing and bit into the flesh and caused a horrible fire and itching. We would rather expose ourselves to being bit by some serpent than to suffer such a torture." In the high country the two men endured chilblains and cracked lips. They were plagued with headaches and temporary blindness from the sun reflecting on the snow. These last afflictions they cured by crying. In the desert they lived on cheese and biscuits along with occasional wild ducks and salt fish. They spent many nights in trees to avoid being surprised by jaguars. The journey, when finally completed, did pay off. The viceroy gave his written authorization and they returned to Quito to carry on the work.

In my notes I had now reached the end of 1737, two and a half years since the start of the Expedition. A year for the journey from France, a year and a half of labor in Peru, and they had still an enormous amount of work to do. The whole project would take seven years. I wonder if they were ever homesick for France, if they had expected the Expedition to be finished in a year or two, if they became discouraged sometimes, and considered abandoning the enterprise. If they did, there is no mention of it in any of the journals. They had all signed up, whether they liked it or not, for the long haul.

EIGHT

DURING THE YEARS OF exploration and scientific research the Frenchmen suffered various illnesses. La Condamine lost consciousness several times for unexplained reasons. He decided it was probably caused by "stretching my neck to see the seconds on my pendulum." By the time he returned to France, he had many symptoms: deafness, partial paralysis, unspecified pains. Bouguer had his gout. Jussieu developed problems with his mental health. However, the members of the Mission never lost their enthusiasm or their feeling of dedication to "the greatest scientific expedition ever made."

Not all the residents of the area viewed the Frenchmen and their work with suspicion. Pedro Maldonado continued to attach himself to the Expedition's projects with boundless enthusiasm, the equal of La Condamine's "burning curiosity." He, too, was young, about thirty, and he and La Condamine were soon companionably doing experiments together, collecting plants, minerals, and bird specimens.

"In the course of our work," La Condamine wrote in his journal, "we received many courtesies from the Creole nobility where some noble Spanish families had come two centuries before and held great territories."

The scientists were invited to country houses; provisions and refreshments were delivered to them while they worked in the mountains. La Condamine drops a few names: Marquis de Maenza, Don Ramon Maldonado, Marquis de Lizes, General Grandmaison of Riobamba.

Since Pedro Maldonado lived in Riobamba, La Condamine was welcome there, along with the other scientists, and there Isabel Grandmaison certainly met them. In 1737, a living base for some of the Expedition members was set up in the welcoming mansion of Sudtrepied, the estate of the Grandmaison family outside the city of Riobamba. It was a magnificent property with every luxury, especially welcome after months of living like dogs in the chilly inhospitable mountains. Isabel, the indulged, cherished daughter of the house, was nine years old. We have no record of her childhood but from later events we must conclude that she was an independent child, adventuresome, curious, eager to know about the world outside of Riobamba or even Peru. The arrival of the young Frenchmen with their tales of camping on volcanoes and, also, of the cultivated life they had left in the great city of Paris, fascinated her.

Young Jean Godin, assistant astronomer, lived for four years as a member of the Grandmaison family, going out for days or weeks at a time to help his cousin Louis study the stars and measure the arc, but returning to watch Isabel grow up. They studied Quechua together, she because she was a natural linguist, he because he needed the language to communicate with Indians in the country. Gradually their common interests expanded. Jean Godin did not always show up for work on the tops of volcanoes; sometimes he remained at the luxurious residence in Riobamba. In 1741, when Isabel turned thirteen, they became engaged.

There was some hesitation by the Grandmaison family—a daughter only thirteen years old marrying a foreigner more than a decade older. But the couple were excited and happy. A big country wedding was planned. All the neighbors and all the elite from Quito came. The members of the French Mission came. They descended from their icy mountain camps, came in from their river expeditions, laid aside their theodolites, barometers, thermometers, measuring rods, and bottles of specimens to help celebrate a marriage that, they agreed, was bound to be happy.

I can imagine the festivities. At the solemn church ceremony General Grandmaison gave the bride away, perhaps with tears in his eyes, for she was only thirteen, barely out of childhood, and the groom, while he was certainly suitable for even a prominent Riobamba family, was older, a foreigner. The general very likely guessed that his favorite daughter would leave Peru and disappear to France forever.

The landowners of Riobamba were keen on parties. Everything was lavish, sophisticated, not at all what the scientists would have expected to find when they arrived in Peru. But by now they were used to it.

The wedding feast would have been preceded by eau-de-vie poured over ice brought from Tungurahua Volcano, drinks accompanied by toasts to the married couple. Delicacies from Europe were served along with the best of local fish, fowl, and meat. The guests listened to plaintive Quechua melodies played on Inca flutes. The best French songs of the day were played on the clavichord, perhaps by Isabel herself. The instrument had been shipped from France and brought up from Guayaquil by muleback. Musicians strummed Spanish guitars with strings made of boa constrictor muscle (better, it was thought, than the intestines of howling monkeys). The guests danced the night away to the strains of the minuet and the fandango. One of the songs they may have sung was prophetic:

J'ai un grand voyage á faire,
Bonjour l'un, bonjour l'autre,
Bonjour, belle que voilà,
C'est votre amant qui demande
Que vous ne l'oublier pas.

[I have a long journey to make,
Good morning to one, good morning another,
Good morning, you beauty over there,
I am your lover who entreats you
Never to forget him.]

Fortunately Isabel and Jean could not foresee the future.

The seven years of the French Expedition were filled, not only with the discoveries of science, but also with tragedies. The death of young Couplet when the party had just arrived was followed not too long after by the news, a major disappointment, that Isaac Newton's theory had been shown to be correct by the findings of the Lapland Expedition. Voltaire, when he heard that Newton had proved the earth to be flattened at the poles, remarked, "Isaac Newton has flattened the world and at the same time has flattened Cassini."

The French Academy acknowledged Newton's findings as correct but instructed the Mission to continue its work, to corroborate the results for use in other studies.

The party moved to Cuenca for their later observations. Dr. Seniergues, the surgeon who had accompanied the Mission from France, not only took care of the medical needs of the scientists but offered his services to the people of the city. He made house calls on various patients, including a prominent citizen whose daughter, Manuela, was the town beauty. She had been engaged, but her fiancé ran off with the mayor's daughter, leaving her not only disconsolate, but destined to remain single. The defection was an insult that made her unmarriageable. Dr. Seniergues became involved in the affair. There was talk—was he her lover? A quarrel arose between the doctor and Manuela's former suitor, insults were exchanged, and a duel was planned but no date was set. The romance became passionate and the couple flaunted their amorous behavior in spite of the vicar's warnings.

It all came to a head on August 29, 1739, at a bullfight in the plaza. A trivial disagreement turned into a full-scale confrontation, with the spectators shouting "Death to the French devils!" Seniergues defended himself with his saber and pistol, but was overcome by the mob and died in a hail of stones.

This brought on La Condamine's most extensive lawsuit, against the doctor's murderers, which took years to settle.

Also at Cuenca, Jussieu, the botanist, suffered the loss of his plant collection of five years when it was destroyed as trash by an ignorant servant. He became depressed and gradually deteriorated, starting with loss of memory and eccentric behavior that increased until, years later, back in France, he lost his reason entirely. A final misfortune occurred when the draftsman, Morainville, died in a fall from a scaffold.

However, it had been a great adventure, one never to be forgotten. Antonio de Ulloa wrote, "In the colossal mountains which we have traversed, men have been privileged to contemplate at the same time all the families of plants and all the stars in the firmament." Individual scientists made important discoveries. Bouguer invented a new instrument to measure the diameter of the sun, the "heliometer." While staying on Mount Pichincha, Jorge Juan discovered a peculiarity of the place: a white rainbow. Jussieu sent a coca plant to Paris where it was grown successfully.

Personal strife among the scientists continued. By 1739, Louis Godin had stopped all communication with La Condamine and Bouguer, refusing to tell them the results of his observations. For his part, La Condamine carried on feuds with almost the whole city of Quito. We have no details as to the reason for these suits, other than those against the doctor's murderers. Nor do we know whether he won or lost them. At one time he had lawsuits going against the grand vicar of Quito, the bishops, the Spanish officers in his own group, and even against the Spanish inquisitor. Later in Paris he published a long account of the Seniergues affair, but I could find nothing on the other incidents. None of the scientists' journals is a day-by-day diary, perhaps fortunately, since the mission lasted for so many years. No doubt the individual members followed their own interests when they were not surveying and "measuring the arc" together. Louis Godin and Bouguer pursued astronomy, Jussieu botany, La Condamine something of everything.

La Condamine in his journal described the good times,

too. He recalled the marriage of a niece of Señor Davalos in Riobamba and the great wedding feast, "the best in all my time in Peru."

He recalled the fiesta put on by a group of Indians, also in Riobamba—a play adapted from Spanish drama with overtones of Moorish history. For this yearly festival, actors rented costumes, lances, and harnesses. It featured horses doing a ballet, but when La Condamine saw it, it featured something more. The Indians had been watching the Frenchmen working, and La Condamine was delighted to see them doing a take-off of the French Mission. They brought onto the scene great quarter-circles of wood and painted paper, took elaborate measurements of the ground, stared at the sky while scratching their heads, and dictated observations to each other that were scribbled down in notebooks. Their caricatures were individual and each scientist recognized himself, especially La Condamine, who noted, "Nothing was more fun in the ten years of my trip. I got such a great desire to laugh that for a while I entirely forgot my most serious business."

Quito seemed to be isolated from the world, but alarms reached the city. In October 1739, war began between Spain and England. This conflict, known as the War of Jenkins's Ear, was precipitated by an English sea captain who appeared in Parliament to show its members one of his ears preserved in a "yellowish liquid" that he said the Spanish had amputated when they captured him in the West Indies. He showed the ugly scar to go with it, and Parliament immediately declared war, especially when Jenkins assured them that his English Majesty's ear was next on the Spanish list.

That same month Admiral Anson was reported to be headed for the Mar del Sur to attack the coast of Chile. The Spaniards, Jorge Juan and Antonio, were urgently sent for to help defend Peru. Later, each of them commanded an armed frigate.

In August 1740, the alarming news arrived from Spain that six English warships were on their way to South America. The viceroy in Lima ordered that the Spanish galleon treasure, usually shipped to Panama, should instead be transported to Guayaquil and thence overland to Quito. On August 9 there appeared in Quito hundreds of mules carrying gold and silver, most of the riches of the New World. The Frenchmen rejoiced because the treasure included letters from Europe that had been only four and a half months on the way.

That autumn the galleon riches arrived in Quito not only from Guayaquil but from Cartagena to the north. On the four-hundred-league route, train after train of mules plodded along carrying a wealth of gold and silver. The journey became a yearly event and in 1742 a mule laden with eighty thousand piastres, or four hundred thousand English pounds worth of gold, fell into the Pisque River about ten leagues from Quito. The river was fifteen feet deep at that point with a shallow ford a little way downstream, so the boxes of gold stayed where they sank. Diving crews went down to search, in vain. The course of the river would have to be changed so that the boxes could be reached, and Louis Godin, no doubt for a sizable share of the treasure, took charge of the work. The river was moved three times, but each time a sudden rush of water ruined the dikes. The gold was never recovered and Louis Godin ran up another big debt.

Alarms of war continued. Jorge Juan and Antonio, each in

charge of a Spanish warship, waited at the Juan Fernandez Islands off of Chile for the coming of Admiral Anson. On November 24, 1741, Anson took the port of Paita south of Guayaquil. "At two o'clock in the morning the *Centurion*, man-of-war, being the Commodore's ship, had entered that harbor, and sent her long-boat ashore with forty armed men, with the advantage of the night, whereby the inhabitants and strangers who happened to be in the place, were wakened from their sleep by the shocking surprise of an invasion, the first notices of which were given by the cries of a negro; so that, filled with confusion and terror, many persons were unable to collect themselves, and most of them had leapt from their beds and fled naked from their houses." This caused alarm in Quito, but Anson passed on along the coast without striking inland. However, that same month sixty men left Quito, most of them released convicts, to join with army recruits from Latacunga, Ambato, and Riobamba, one hundred and eighty in all. The governor and captain general of Quito marched at the head of the militia.

Meanwhile, La Condamine went on with his experiments and investigations. That was all very well but, as usual, he could not resist seeking publicity. This led to the controversial affair of "the pyramids of the moon." The idea was to perpetuate the memory of the French Geodesic Mission with a monument. La Condamine decided, without consulting the government of Quito, to build a pyramid at each end of the original line of measurement of the arc, close to the equator. The possibility of a memorial had been discussed with the French Academy of Science before the Expedition started, and the plan had been approved with the actual design left to La Condamine.

He set to work. The project was difficult. To bring water to the arid land where the monuments would be erected, a canal two leagues long had to be constructed. Then an oven must be made to bake the bricks. Slabs of stone for the inscriptions were laboriously quarried and brought from a remote section of the Andes. The Indians who made the inscriptions on the pyramid had to copy each letter from a drawing since they were illiterate. Frequently, tired of the job, they disappeared. At one line a day, the inscriptions took six weeks of work. Then the stone pyramids were not solid; wooden bases had to be added.

Finally, the work was completed. No sooner was it done, however, than an official storm broke out. The pyramids held the names of the French scientists and on top of each monument, as decoration, was engraved a fleur-de-lys. The authorities in Quito were enraged. First, the names of the Spaniards, the naval officers Jorge Juan Santacilla and Antonio de Ulloa, who had been assigned to the Expedition by the king of Spain, were omitted. Weren't they members of the Mission? Of course they were! Then, the ultimate insult, the fleur-de-lys that topped the monuments was an emblem of France, as everyone knew. French sovereignty was certainly not accepted in the audiencia of Quito. The pyramids were destroyed.

As Hugot, the French watchmaker, remarked when he saw the construction, "Pyramids here? That's like putting pyramids on the moon!"

The scientific work, meanwhile, went on uninterrupted. Finally, in March 1743, the whole project was completed, the arc was measured, the Expedition members were free at last to go home. The final observations were made at Tarqui, near Cuenca. Jean Godin rode there from Riobamba to take part in the finish.

Very likely it was at this time that he began discussing with La Condamine the project of going back to France down the Amazon to the Atlantic and thence by ship, a route seldom traveled by Europeans, except the occasional missionary. It was a journey full of dangers from the unknown jungle, the Indians, the rivers to be traversed, the wild animals to be encountered, but it was a journey of unrivaled adventure. It is no surprise that La Condamine, with his "burning curiosity," would choose this way, and Jean Godin no doubt was fired with the same enthusiasm. However, it involved also Jean's wife, Isabel. It is an interesting glimpse of her character that she apparently agreed unhesitatingly to go along. For an eighteenth-century woman of society, such a journey was unheard of. At least La Condamine and Maldonado would go ahead and blaze the way. She was pregnant and the trip must wait until the baby was born. La Condamine would alert the missions and send back word of the details of his trip.

❦

The results of the measurements of the arc were sent off to the Academy. They proved that Isaac Newton's theory of the earth's shape was correct. Voltaire wrote of the French Expedition:

> *Vous avez trouvé par de longs ennuis*
> *Ce que Newton trouva sans sortir de chez lui.*

[You have found through tedious work
What Newton discovered without leaving home.]

After the Expedition returned to Paris, Bouguer and La Condamine could not agree in their interpretation of their findings, because they used two baselines and lacked computing techniques. The mean result of their observations was taken and combined with the results of the Lapland Expedition. Later on, these arc measurements would be accepted by the French government as an official unit of measurement. In 1791, the French National Assembly adopted a new length unit, the meter, and defined it as 1:10,000,000 part of the meridian quadrant from the equator to the pole along the meridian running through Paris.

NINE

IT WAS TIME AT last to go home to France. La Condamine wrote:
"In order to multiply the chances of observations we had
agreed for a long time, M. Godin, M. Bouguer and I, to return
by different routes. I was determined to choose an almost
unknown way, which I was sure no one would envy me; it was
that of the River of the Amazons, which crosses the whole
continent . . . from west to east, and which is called, with
reason, the greatest river in the world. I planned to make this
a useful trip by making a map of the river and by collecting
every sort of observation . . . in a country so little known."

Maldonado, against the advice of his family and friends,
agreed to go along. At Cayenne on the Atlantic, they would
catch the king's ship that left once a year for France.

I recalled my first trip to South America some years ago
when I went with friends to take a look at the Amazon. We

flew from Lima to Iquitos. The earth, viewed from the plane, was a huge patchwork in brilliant shades of green and brown. Brown streams meandered through areas of green jungle. A few white clouds cast darker shadows on the pattern. No sign appeared of any life. Ten thousand years ago the view would have been the same if there had been airplanes flying over it. I know that the rainforest is threatened if not doomed, but an immense area is still apparently untouched.

We circled, descended, and landed at Iquitos. This rundown river port, stranded between memories of the rubber boom and dreams of future tourists, straggles along the bank of the brown, monotonous width of the Amazon. I recall that Iquitos did not exist when La Condamine and Maldonado came this way. It was the product of the rubber bonanza much later. However, during his voyage down the river, La Condamine discovered that rubber would stretch, was waterproof, and could be made into receptacles and all kinds of things. He took samples back to Paris and so perhaps I could call him the father of the rubber boom.

We sat under the thatched roof of the motorboat that would take us downriver to the lodge where we planned to spend a few days. Some power-driven canoes traveled up and down the river, and other simpler craft worked their way along with native rowers. Shacks clung to the bank here and there. We kept to the middle of the river where the current helped us downstream, and the shores were very far away. I couldn't see any details except a tiny figure of a man launching a canoe, and at another spot a group of people on the beach hauling in a net. I looked over the side as our boat chugged along, but the water was too brown and mud-laden to make out anything below the surface.

"There are paiche fish on the bottom," our boatman said,

jerking the wheel to avoid a floating island of debris. "Some of them are two meters long." He took his hands off the wheel to show us, and the boat slewed around. "They'll give you some for dinner at the lodge."

The lodge, when we reached it, was in the high style of primitive retreats for fastidious campers. Private cabins perched on stilts against the rainy season floods. Meticulous screening kept out the omnivorous insects. The lodge served carefully-simple meals featuring local delicacies, paiche fish among them.

The next day we were taken for a walk through the jungle to a settlement of Yagua Indians, who had changed into grass skirts for our benefit. The old chief was still a dead shot at a target with his blowgun, although I suppose the arrows are not coated with curare these days. The children spoke some Spanish and went to school where they learned to read and write.

This was not the jungle as La Condamine or Isabel Godin knew it in the eighteenth century. Whether the natives have benefited from their entry into civilization, I do not know. That is a moot point. The Yaguas have a good little business going in necklaces of colored stones, feathers, and piranha teeth.

On the plane back to Lima I thought about the history of the great river, from the time when Columbus first wrote to Queen Isabella that the mouth of the Orinoco was the gateway to paradise. The Amazon was first discovered by Vicente Yañez Pinzon in 1499. He had commanded the ship *Nina* under Columbus, and now while looking for new countries he came upon the mouth of the river. It was not too difficult to find, for the current carries so much silt, mud, and debris out into the ocean that it colors the water brown for a hundred miles. Yañez Pinzon called the new river Rio

Santa Maria de la Mar Dulce and believed himself to be in India beyond the Ganges. He was sure that he had sailed near to the great "city" of Cathay.

Soon the location of the rivers was better understood, but it was centuries before the Amazon was fully explored; the difficulties were too great.

When early travelers set out to go from the high Andes to the Atlantic Ocean by way of the river Amazonas, they were beset with hardships. The friar Gaspar de Carvajal recorded the sufferings of Francisco Orellana and his men, in 1541 the first to embark on such a journey. They became so weak with hunger that they crawled on all fours unearthing roots to eat. Some of them went mad after devouring poisonous plants.

The historian Oviedo, a member of the expedition, re-called it later: "In the meantime lacking other victuals, we were eating leather from the seats and bows of saddles and also from game [on the outside] of the chests or hampers whose cover was made of it, in which we were transporting the little clothing and bedding that we had, and a few tapir skins, not to mention the soles and [even old] shoes that could be found among the members of the party; and though there was no source other than hunger itself, this latter created a . . . taste [for these things] and such an appetite that was to a point where we could stand it no longer these dishes of a sort so new were tolerated in order that this wretched flesh of ours might be sustained."

Next to starvation came the plague of mosquitoes: "Men on watch or building the brigantine worked for one hour when it was necessary for another man or even two to drive away the mosquitoes by means of a pair of fans made out of feathers which the Indians gave us. . . . A man could not even eat except when another one fanned the mosquitoes away from him."

However, interest in the new continent continued to run high. Francisco Pizarro had publicized the wonders and riches of the land beyond the Amazon that he had seen. Upon his return to Spain, he followed Charles V from court to court for three years to petition the crown for the official powers to conquer the new "Peru." He carried with him hampers of gold and silver ornaments, cloth woven from vicuña wool, "such a quality unseen in Spain," and three live llamas. Word spread that in this faraway country the natives were gentle, the dogs were barkless, people drank from cups of gold, and diamonds could be picked up in the streets.

A century later, in 1637, the Portuguese leader Pedro Texeira set out to explore the river. He went upstream, along with a party of seventy soldiers, one thousand two hundred native bowmen and rowers, and miscellaneous women and slaves—a total of two thousand people traveling in forty-five canoes. A year later they reached Quito, and their arrival was celebrated with processions and bullfights. They had good tales to tell of the Encabellados, the "longhairs," the Omaguas, the "flatheads," and the dwarfs whose feet grew backwards. Over in Europe tales of the new land proliferated, one writer even speaking of elephants. The unknown expanse of jungle set the imaginations of illustrators afire. Pictures showed men riding rebellious alligators, tigers bounding over tall trees, and snakes crushing entire boat crews in their coils.

One story told of the fabled kingdom of El Dorado and the Golden Man, where gold was so common that the king wore only a coating of gold dust, which was washed from his body every night and replaced with a fresh coat the next morning. The monarch considered gold dust more handsome than any suit of clothes. As for owning gold plates and ornaments— much too awkward, actually vulgar.

An Indian legend told of the lake of Guatavita, high in the Andes, where a princess threw herself into the water, leaving her prince to mourn. He spent many months beside the lake. Finally he consulted a sorcerer who instructed him to dive into the icy water. On coming up he swam to shore and gave the news: "The princess lives! She sits in a palace more beautiful than ours, where she is happy." Twice a year pilgrims came to the lake. They smeared the body of their chief with balsamic resin, blew gold dust on it, and took him to the center of the lake by raft. He tossed gold, emeralds, and precious images into the water, then immersed himself until the gold dust was washed away. Oviedo wrote: "I would rather have the sweepings from the chamber of this monarch than that of the great melting establishments in Peru."

Then there were the Amazons, the race of women living their independent lives on the great river. Early explorers insisted they had seen them, giving convincing details. The chronicler Carvajal described them as "very white and tall and having hair long and braided and wound about the head. They are very robust and go about naked, but with their privy parts covered. With their bows and arrows in their hands they do as much fighting as ten Indian men."

They lived on a lake called "Mansion of the Sun," so it was reported, because the sun sank into it. They lived a seven-day journey into the interior, in seventy villages. Their houses were of stone. The upper-class women ate from utensils of gold and silver while the lower classes used wood or clay. They wore blankets of fine llama wool, girded about them from the breasts down, thrown over one shoulder or clasped together in front like a cloak. They wore crowns of gold as wide as two fingers and rode about on "camels."

The Amazons, according to the stories, made war on

surrounding tribes and captured husbands, but they kept these men with them for a short time only. Other reports had the men turning up voluntarily, once a year, in April. Any male Indian, according to these accounts, must depart at sundown. The Amazons raised their female children, but male babies were returned to their fathers, alive or, according to some chroniclers, dead. On parting from their men the women gave them gifts of green jadelike stones, which were called Amazon stones.

Even in La Condamine's day these stones were sometimes carried by traveling friars who had been among the jungle Indians. The stones were said to cure "nephritic colic" and epilepsy.

These strange women were malevolent in some unspecific way. "The Indians told us that anyone who should take it into his head to go down to the country of these women was destined to go a boy and return an old man."

It would be hard to believe that the narrators had made up all the details. Later, explorers may have proved these tales to have no basis in fact, but the rumors persisted for many years, well into the eighteenth century when La Condamine made his journey.

Gradually, missions had sprung up along the four thousand miles of river basin and its tributaries. These were manned by men of God, who were often well meaning, but on occasion were men of mammon who mistreated the Indians and made the Indians' little centers of civilization into kingdoms where they were sole rulers. Wonders were no longer expected, but a fog of mystery still hung over the Amazon. No one had yet explored the area; no one had looked with a practical eye on what this huge land contained.

TEN

THERE WERE THREE WAYS to reach the Amazon from Quito: in the north by the Napo River, a middle route by the Pastaza, and the southern one by the Loja River and the Marañon. This last one was a longer journey and a rough one, where it rained nearly every day of the year, and where Europeans almost never went because of the dangerous Pongo Rapids. That was the way La Condamine chose. He had preserved his boyhood love of adventure, although he was now forty years old and had already had a lifetime's worth of dangerous undertakings. I can hear him saying, as he talked to some friar who had made the trip, "The Pongo Rapids. Very risky you say? That's the route for me. I didn't come to Peru to relax. I represent the French Academy and have my work to do."

La Condamine's preparations were soon made. He found good markets for the scientific instruments and heavy equipment. He sold his big tent, setting it up in the main square in Quito, "where ladies and other curious people came to see it." It was bought by a man for hunting trips.

I can imagine the tent set up nowadays, with all the traffic shooed out of the Plaza, and La Condamine standing there in his traveling outfit, probably wool trousers and poncho, ready to answer questions from the waiting reporters and television crews.

Just before he left Quito, his lodgings were broken into and his money and papers stolen, including, I suppose, the profits from his equipment sale. He got back most of the papers but not the money. Thinking of the dangers of the Pongo Rapids, he made an extract of his most important notes and also wrote his will.

Maldonado started out by the Pastaza route and La Condamine followed shortly, taking four months to go from Tarqui over the mountains to the Loja River, three hundred miles south of Riobamba. One reason he chose the southern river route was because he had discovered quinine trees there and wanted to examine them again. At Loja he hired guides and proceeded on horseback to the Marañon. It rained constantly, but La Condamine was excited by the thought of navigating the famous Pongo straits. He wrote, "It was mostly to know for myself this strait, which was spoken of in Quito with admiration mixed with fear, and to understand for my map the whole navigable portion of the river, that I chose the last route."

La Condamine delighted in every mile of his prolonged river trip. Details fascinated him, not only scientific discoveries but the everyday adventures of the voyage. He described the bridges made of strong vines, or lianas:

> These lianas interlaced in a network, form a gallery in the air from one bank to the other, suspended from two great cables of the same materials, the ends of which are attached at each side to tree branches. The whole looks

like a fishnet, or better still, an Indian hammock stretched from one side to the other of the river. As the mesh of this netting is very large and one's feet may go through it, they have stretched some reeds in the bottom of this cradle to serve as a floor. Evidently the weight alone of all this fabric, and still more the weight of anyone crossing it, makes the whole thing take a sharp curve. . . and anyone passing over it when he is in the middle, or when there is wind, finds himself exposed to a great swinging. One can understand that such a bridge, sometimes more than thirty toises long [one hundred eighty feet], is frightening at first sight. However, the Indians, who are by nature intrepid, cross it running with all the baggage and with the cargo of the mules who have to swim the river. They laugh at a traveler who hesitates, who is ashamed of showing less courage than they.

He described his scientific work in detail from day to day: "I took soundings and measured geometrically the width of the river and of the other rivers which emptied into it; I took a noon sight of the sun almost every day, and I often observed its size when it rose and when it set; I also set up the barometer in every place where I stopped."

He had an equal curiosity about new plants, strange animals and birds, tribes of Indians encountered along the way.

Fortunately he had the scientist's eye for facts and respect for truth. I wonder what he thought of some of the reports that had emerged from this unexplored region over the years. They featured huge giants who used trees for walking sticks; serpents that could kill a man with their breath; all sorts of monstrous creatures frequenting the jungle and the rivers. There were some astonishing animals in real life. The opossum was a surprise to the early conquistadors, who described it as having "the fore part of a fox, hind part of a monkey, the feet of an ape, the ears of a bat." An opossum was dispatched to Seville and then sent on to Grenada so that the king and queen might see it.

The perilous liana bridges were not the only problem on the land part of La Condamine's journey.

> From Loxa to Jaen one crosses the last slopes of the cordillera. . . . One walks almost always in the woods, where it rains every day during eleven and sometimes twelve months of the year; it isn't possible to dry anything. The baskets covered with cowhide, which are the traveling cases of the country, rot and give off an insupportable odor.
>
> I passed twenty-one times through fords along the torrent of the Chuchunga, and crossed a final time by boat; the mules, on approaching a crossing, threw themselves into the water and swam all laden; my instruments, my books, my papers, all were wet.

Before reaching the Pongo he had his share of adventures. He met some Jibaro Indians, formerly Christians, who had revolted against the Spaniards who forced them to work in the gold mines. They retired into the inaccessible forest from which they sallied to attack travelers and "impede navigation." This is the tribe that were later known as headhunters, their reputation for savagery continuing until almost the present time. They did, however, leave La Condamine and his Indian helpers alone.

More frightening was being trapped in a whirlpool. This was well before he reached the Pongo, when he was traveling on a smallish balsa.

> The river stopped by a cliff, which it goes over perpendicularly, is obliged to turn suddenly, making a right angle.

The shock of the water with all the speed acquired by the narrowing of the channel, has hollowed out a deep hole where the water at the edge of the river is retained, cast aside by the speed of the current in the middle. My raft, . . . pushed by the current in this spot, turned around and around for an hour and some minutes. The water, circling, carried me towards the middle of the river, where the meeting of the currents formed waves which would surely have submerged a canoe, but I was always pushed back by the violence of the current into the depths of the hole, from which I was pulled by the skill of four Indians, whom I had kept with me in a small canoe, for any eventuality. These, with difficulty, threw me some vines from a rock . . . with which they towed the balsa until it was again in the channel.

One night, after he had carefully moored his balsa to the riverbank, he fell asleep. He had not known that the stream receded as much as twenty-five feet in thirty-six hours. "In the middle of the night," he wrote, "a big branch of a tree became tangled with the wood of my raft which it penetrated more and more as the level of the river went down. I was at the point, if I had not wakened, of resting with the raft suspended in the air on a tree branch, where the least that could have happened to me was to lose my journals and the notes of my observations. I found a way to extricate myself with difficulty."

The passage of the Pongo was comparatively easy. La Condamine had an especially large, stout balsa built, and made the descent successfully.

Near the Pongo falls, the waters seem to hurl themselves and strike the rocks causing a terrifying noise.

On the 12th of July at noon, I cast the raft adrift . . . in less than an hour I found myself transported to Borja, three leagues below Sant-Iago. In the narrowest part I think we made two toises [about twelve feet] per second.

On the way I was hurled two or three times roughly against the rocks; it would have been terrifying if I had not been warned. A canoe would break a thousand times . . . and they showed me in passing the place where the governor of Maynas had died; but since the pieces of a raft are not nailed . . . the flexibility of the vines used to fasten it together deaden the blows and one need not take any precaution against blows to the raft.

In Borja I encountered a new world, with no relation to human beings, a sea of fresh water, surrounded by a labyrinth of lakes, rivers, and canals and penetrated in all directions by the obscurity of an immense forest . . . I saw new plants, new animals, new races of men. After being accustomed for seven years to mountains lost among the clouds, I could not grow tired of looking around the horizon. . . . To that crowd of varied objects, which diversifies the cultivated country around Quito, succeeded a uniform aspect: of water, of verdure, and nothing else. One treads on the earth without seeing it, it is so covered with tufted grass, plants and brushwood, that it would require much work to uncover the space of one foot.

We, in these modern times, can seldom be the first tourists anywhere: in the mountains, in the jungles, or on the rivers. Yet many of us have a secret hankering to be explorers, to visit the world as it used to be. This was part of my interest in Isabel. She had seen things that I would never see, walked where no human being had been before. The manager of my hotel in Cuenca spotted me as such a person and eagerly provided brochures. I read about the *Floatel*, a first-class mobile lodging that would ferry groups of tourists down the Napo River through the jungle, provided the water was deep enough. (I wondered what would be offered if it wasn't.) Then there would be a hike into the forest and a night in a first-class jungle dormitory. The brochure admitted that the tourists would not see any animals since they do not appear to large groups of human beings. On the other hand, the expedition members could all swing along monkey-fashion by lianas, vines more than strong enough to support a tour group, and know that the beasts in the jungle were watching, no doubt with amazement. Before heading home there would be a stop for a photo opportunity at a small private zoo, so the travelers could tell stay-at-homes of their adventures.

The second brochure offered three days among the head-hunters. My guidebook told me that nowadays it would be tactless to ask them about headhunting, but the brochure had other suggestions. After visiting a haunt of these Indians, the brochure guaranteed that each visitor would come back with his own head. He could bring another head as a souvenir. It would be the shrunken head of a monkey that takes three days to prepare (the visitor could watch this process) and would be remarkably lifelike. So much for the posters I had admired in Quito, which stated that no wild animals can be legally killed in Ecuador.

The manager was surprised that I said no to both sugges-tions.

La Condamine met various tribes of Indians as he proceeded down the Marañon to the Amazon. He was impressed with

"Savages called Yameos: They talk while inhaling and sound almost no vowels. They have words which we could not write with less than ten syllables; and when they pronounce them they seem to have only three or four. Poettarrarorincouroac means the number three. Happily for anyone dealing with them, their arithmetic does not go any further."

He learned that the Omaguas, the "flatheads," placed the heads of newborn infants between two boards to make them flat so that they "will resemble the full moon."

At Pevas the Indians wore animal and fish bones passed through their nostrils and lips, put brightly colored feathers in holes in their cheeks, and through their enormously stretched earlobes placed tufts of grass and flowers as earrings.

La Condamine carried a map showing where the Spanish missions were along the way, the races of Indians and their various languages. At the town of Lagunas he met Maldonado, who had been waiting there six weeks. Maldonado had come down the middle route, using the Pastaza River north of La Condamine's river passage. At the confluence of the Pastaza and the Marañon he left a message nailed to a tree: "I will meet you at Las Lagunas on the River Huellaga." This he left in May; La Condamine came that way in July and picked it off the tree.

I wish La Condamine were here so that I could ask him about that message, which remained readable from May to July. It was "nailed to a tree" in a place where the rains were almost continuous. Not paper then, but what?

As La Condamine noted, Maldonado "had made interesting observations during his trip, using a compass and a portable sundial, and he had thus been able to chart the course of the Pastaza." The two friends went on their way together, no doubt happy to be able to exchange thoughts on the new world they were passing through.

La Condamine continued to be interested in the possibilities of rubber. "When it is fresh, they shape it with moulds into whatever form they want; it is impenetrable to water; but what is the most remarkable is its great elasticity. They make bottles, and balls which flatten out when pressed and afterwards return to their former shape."

He checked up on the stories of El Dorado and the River of Gold. There were many credible accounts, but they were the stuff of history and legend. "Many witnesses make one believe the truth of the account; however the river, the lake, the gold mine . . . even the Village of Gold, attested to by the deposition of so many witnesses, all has disappeared like an enchanted palace, and in the places where these things were even their memory is lost."

The Amazons were equally elusive. "In the course of our navigation, we questioned the Indians of different tribes, and we learned from them whether they had any knowledge of the warlike women whom Orellana claimed to have encountered and with whom he fought, and asked if it was true that they lived far from men, receiving them only once a year. . . . Everyone said that yes, their fathers had encountered such women, adding a thousand details too long to repeat, which all tend to confirm that there had been in this continent a republic of women who lived alone . . . and that they had retreated towards the north of the interior, by the river Negro or perhaps some other river along the Marañon." Everything, La Condamine felt, pointed to the existence of Amazons in times past. Perhaps, however, they had given up their tribal customs, or perhaps they had been conquered by another tribe, or possibly, tired of their solitude, the daughters had at last forgotten their mothers' hatred of men. "Therefore," he concluded, "while we no longer find today actual traces of this Women's Republic, that is still not enough to prove that it never existed."

Not only did La Condamine, and Maldonado when they had met, make measurements of the width and depth of the rivers and the speed of the current in each, but they drew a map of the Amazon and its maze of tributaries so nearly correct that it has been little changed in the centuries since then.

La Condamine made other interesting discoveries. He found that the Indians paralyzed fish with the plant verbasco, containing the chemical rotenone, which has since been much used as an insecticide. He noted how animals died when shot with poison-tipped arrows, and heard it said that their meat could be safely eaten if sugar was taken immediately afterward. To test this on himself, he killed a chicken using a poisoned arrow, ate a piece, swallowed sugar at once, and "didn't feel at all sick."

La Condamine and Maldonado had a routine trip down the river, as did Jean Godin so far as we know. Isabel's dreadful journey was the result of the smallpox epidemic in Canelos, which made it impossible to get the necessary transportation.

As the two friends descended the river they saw signs of encroaching civilization: "At St. Paul we began to see instead of houses and churches made of reeds, chapels and presbyteries of masonry . . . and of brick, and walls properly whitewashed. We were also agreeably surprised, to see in the middle of these deserts, chemises of cloth from Brittany on all the Indian women, boxes with iron fittings, and iron keys for the houses, and to notice needles, little mirrors, knives and combs from Europe which the Indians obtain . . .

in Para where they go to sell cacao which they gather from the river banks."

The shipping was more frequent and the vessels larger. There were canoes or "brigantines" using a tree trunk for the center of the hull and adding side boards for height. La Condamine saw some sixty feet long, seven feet wide and three and a half feet deep, and heard of even larger craft with as many as forty rowers. Most boats had two masts with sails that could go upstream easily when the winds were right.

The scientists stopped to rest at a string of missions along the river, first Spanish ones and later Portuguese. They were received everywhere with courtesy and offers of assistance. At each stop La Condamine told the friars that soon his friend Jean Godin would come down the river with his wife Isabel. These messages were remembered years later.

La Condamine and Maldonado reached Para on the Atlantic coast in only two months, a quick passage. Here they separated. Maldonado took ship for London. La Condamine went up the coast to Cayenne where he stayed several months, then on to Surinam to catch a Dutch ship for the passage home to Europe. On February 23, in the year 1745, he arrived at Paris, almost ten years after he had left it.

La Condamine's account of his river journey is admirably concise. It is tantalizing, however, that he often abruptly changes the subject when describing native tribes, scenery, and the like, explaining that he must stick to scientific information and save many curious details of his travels for private meetings of the Academy.

He describes at the end of his account coatis, various kinds of monkeys, coral snakes and rattlers, electric eels, bats, toucans, hummingbirds, and parrots. The anteater, the sloth, the armadillo, all are listed.

He describes tigers (jaguars) and their method of attacking crocodiles by clawing their eyes, on which the crocodile would drag the animal into the water where either one might win the contest.

He tells how the Indians on the banks of the Oyapok River change the coloring of parrots "by pulling out their feathers and rubbing them with the blood of certain ants . . . it is not unusual to see a bird grow red or yellow feathers instead of the green ones which had been plucked."

The great condors, he writes, can swoop down on a lamb or even a tiny child. The Indians told him that they made as bait a child's figure out of extremely sticky clay. The condor would swoop down, take it in his talons, and be unable to disengage himself.

La Condamine was particularly interested in a small monkey given him by the governor of Para, the only one of its kind seen in the country. He kept it as a pet to take home to France, and I get the impression that he loved the little animal. He must often have been lonely during the ten years of the Expedition, punctuated by arguments with his colleagues and lawsuits that he probably did not win, since they were against foreigners in a strange country. He did have courage and perhaps even enjoyed litigation. It is hard to imagine anyone bringing suit in a Spanish colony against the Inquisition itself!

He describes the monkey in detail:

"The hair on its body was silver, the color of beautiful blond hair, that of its tail a lustrous chestnut color, almost black. It had another remarkable characteristic; its ears, its cheeks, and its nose were such a bright vermillion that it was hard to believe that the color was natural. I kept him for a year, and he was still living when I was writing this almost in sight of the French coast, where I would like to have brought him alive. In spite of the care I constantly took to keep him from the cold, the severity of the season probably caused his death."

Now that his pet was dead, he became another of La Condamine's scientific specimens. "Since I had no means on the ship to dry him in the oven, such as Monsieur de Reaumur had thought of for preserving birds, all I could do was preserve him in eau-de-vie, which will perhaps be enough to show that I didn't exaggerate at all in my description."

If La Condamine were writing his account for today's readers perhaps he would liven his scientific descriptions by telling us where and how along the great river he encountered the crocodile, the coral snake, the electric eels, and the jaguars. No doubt in his private meetings with confreres at the Academy he had many fascinating details to relate.

ELEVEN

Armadilio

LA CONDAMINE SEPARATED FROM Maldonado when they reached the mouth of the Amazon and headed along the coast to Guiana and Surinam. From there he took ship to Europe and reached France in 1745. Meanwhile, other members of the French Geodesic Mission made their various ways home with adventures along the way.

Pedro Maldonado, after accompanying La Condamine on the Amazon journey, traveled to London, where he was admired and feted and elected to membership in the Royal Society. A productive scientific career lay ahead, the future for which he had left Riobamba. However, he had not the resistance of Europeans to current diseases. He caught measles and died on November 17, 1748, at the age of forty. He was buried in St. James's Church, Piccadilly.

Don Jorge Juan shipped from South America for his return to Spain on the French vessel *Délivrance*, in 1744. Don Antonio de Ulloa took passage at the same time on a companion vessel, *Lys*. They traveled separately in case one of the ships should be lost. The two vessels doubled the Horn and reached Brazil on June 10, 1744. As usual, there was a war on, in this case England against France. The French ships left the coast and encountered two English warships, the *Prince Frederick* and the *Duke*. They engaged and the *Délivrance* was captured. Jorge Juan threw his packet of secret orders from Spain overboard but kept his scientific papers from the Geodesic Expedition. He was stripped and searched and the papers taken from him. He was then sent to England and confined in a prison at the entrance to Portsmouth harbor. However, there he was treated as befitted a gentleman of the times, being invited to eat at the table of Captain Brett of the *Sunderland*, which was berthed close by.

Captain Brett encouraged him to send a petition to the Duke of Bedford, First Lord of the Admiralty, seeking to get back his scientific papers. The duke replied promptly that he was "not at war with the arts and sciences or their professors." Jorge Juan then journeyed to London where the papers were returned and he was given his freedom. He was elected to the Royal Society and made much of in London. After his visit there he embarked at Falmouth on the packet boat and reached Madrid July 26, 1746, two years after his capture.

La Condamine, ever given to correspondence, wrote in 1774 to "Monsieur M****," who had inquired about the fate of the members of the Expedition.

I could answer you with this verse from Virgil:

"In this vast ocean, escaped from shipwreck,
Some few saved themselves by swimming."

Of those who survived the years in Peru, M. Bouguer died in 1758 of an abscess of the liver. Louis Godin, who moved to Spain, became Director of the Marine Academy at Cadiz. Although he was younger than Bouguer, he survived him by only two years. M. Hugo, the watch-maker, married in Quito and remained there. No word has been heard from him for more than fifteen years. Don Jorge Juan became, after his return from England, Commandant of Marines and later Ambassador to Madrid. He just died, in Madrid, of apoplexy.

Jussieu had returned to France only a couple of years earlier, in 1772, after being detained in Quito by the audiencia to practice his profession of medicine during a smallpox epidemic there. He had now completely lost his memory, and La Condamine made the wry comment: "I don't know if the two of us can be counted as one living person. My deafness, which started in America, has become severe, and for the last five years I have lost external feeling in the lower part of my body, of which I only know the existence because of pain when the weather changes. Thus, of the voyagers to the Torrid zone, not counting our servants, there remain only Don Antonio de Ulloa, squadron chief in the Spanish navy and former Governor of Louisiana, and M. Godin des Odonais who has just arrived at Paris after an absence of thirty-eight years. He gave me last August the story of his wife's journey (I knew her from her childhood), whose adventures I had known only from vague rumor."

La Condamine himself, from the time he arrived home in 1745, continued to write, to attend meetings of the Academy of Sciences, and to talk at length on all subjects. In 1757, when he was fifty-six, he made a trip to Rome to procure papal dispensation to marry his niece, who was twenty years younger, "so that he could be well taken care of." This was granted.

By 1758 he was so deaf he needed an ear trumpet and his left leg was paralyzed, making it hard to attend Academy meetings. He treated the paralysis with electric charges and composed songs to forget his pain. In 1759, the French Academy made him one of their "forty immortals" and a satirical epigramme went the rounds of the Paris salons:

La Condamine est aujourd'hui
Reçu dans la troupe immortelle;
Il est bien sourd; tant mieux pour lui;
Mais non muet; tant pis pour elle.

[Today the Immortal group of Forty
Received La Condamine;
He's very deaf; for him that's fine;
But he's not mute—poor group of Forty.]

Early in 1774 La Condamine was to have an operation, which he approached with his usual insatiable curiosity, asking to have the surgery done slowly (in those days before anesthetics) so that he could watch the details and tell the Academy about it. He died on February 4, a few days after the surgery.

TWELVE

AFTER THEIR MARRIAGE IN 1741 Jean and Isabel Godin lived on the Grandmaison estate outside Riobamba. They continued to delay their departure for France, waiting through Isabel's repeated pregnancies. Jean managed the property for his in-laws; Isabel passed the days as she always had in the big house. Few records have come down of those years, for they were quiet ones. Life went on as usual in the town of Riobamba. Jean busied himself riding around the property checking on the planting, the harvest, and the care of cattle and sheep. This life suited him far better than camping on frozen volcanoes with his cousin Louis, holding a telescope, noting down findings, making a surveyor's measurements for the famous "arc," and hauling tents from peak to peak. He passed the years contentedly with his wife Isabel as she grew from a very young, lovely girl to a strong and beautiful woman.

Not everything at the Grandmaison estate was happy. Isabel became pregnant three times before she was twenty, and each time the baby died of one of the tropical diseases that were always waiting to decimate the child population: smallpox, malaria, yellow fever, dysentery. In her sorrow for the death of her children, Isabel grew closer to her husband. They continued to be as happy with one another as they had been on their wedding day.

Eventually word came through that La Condamine's journey down the Amazon had been successful, and no doubt Jean and Isabel spent many hours planning their descent of the rivers, the voyage to France, the reunion with Jean's family and friends, and Isabel's first encounter with a different culture.

I studied my copy of the drawing of Isabel Godin, which appeared a century later in the *Magasin Pittoresque* in Paris, along with a lively story of her adventures. The drawing was done from an oil painting that Jean sent home to Saint-Amand Montrond. If his family were expecting the portrait of a strange, exotic woman from a far land, they were reassured. She looks like any European lady of the eighteenth century. Her dress and jewelry show her to be upper-class. She sits at a desk and fingers an unopened fan, surely a pose suggested by the artist. However, looking at her closely, I think some hint comes through of strength of mind and resolution.

The years from 1741 to 1748 were marked by a series of wars that convulsed Europe and parts of the New World. However, aside from the conscripts sent to the army from Quito and the gold trains arriving there, the wars left the city untouched. Riobamba, some 125 miles south of Quito, was quiet.

The most important local happening was the eruption of the Cotopaxi Volcano in 1744, a cataclysm still listed among important world events. Spectators described cataracts of fire and blocks of ice rumbling down the slopes. The noise was deafening. The sky darkened, clouds of ash drifted overhead. The sun turned green and the sky became blood red, then the color of tarnished copper, then of polished brass. Ashes littered the fields and the cattle went wild with fear. The sky was dark all the way to the ocean. The volcano was far enough away from Riobamba that the town was not endangered, but in Latacunga a few miles to the north many died in a torrent of lava and ashes.

The visiting French astronomers had introduced Quito and Riobamba society to the stars and planets. Everyone took an interest in any new celestial phenomenon. The appearance of a large comet with six tails led to a hairstyle among the ladies called "La Cometa," which featured six braids. Society recovered from its Gallic craze although French wines and brandies remained popular. At dances where, for a while, everyone had tried to converse in fine French, Castilian again became the language of choice. Coq au vin was replaced on menus by hornado, a suckling pig baked whole with a bell pepper for its mouth and two chili peppers for eyes. The lively fandango replaced the courtly minuet.

Quito was subject, during those years, to repeated epidemics. In 1744 a "malignant pestilential fever" took the lives of eight thousand citizens and in 1745 smallpox appeared (it was said to turn up at fourteen-year intervals), lasted six months and caused many deaths. The botanist Jussieu, who was also a doctor, was much in demand to treat patients, so much so that the Quito government refused to allow him to leave the city and return to France. He kept trying to get permission to go to Canelos, the "City of Cinnamon Trees," for botanical research. He finally did make a trip there, in 1747, going by way of the volcano

Tungurahua. He had planned to go on down the Amazon, but was ordered by the Spanish authorities to return to Quito, bringing back some instruments and other gear belonging to the Academy. Jean and Isabel must have heard Jussieu's description of the rough journey to Canelos and beyond.

Nothing they heard, however, made them change their plans. They simply had to delay their departure.

During those years Jean thought often of France. Nothing in colonial Riobamba, no matter how luxurious or cultured, could make up for the amenities of Paris. No doubt he described these often to Isabel. She perhaps became obsessed with thoughts of a country at the very center of the civilized world, where her husband would show her everything and where, too, he would show her off to his family and friends. However, the journey was delayed because of Isabel's pregnancies and the infant deaths that followed. A long time passed after La Condamine left word at the Amazon missions that his friends the Godins would be coming that way.

Finally, in 1748, Jean's father died in France and pressing business matters made it essential for him to go at once, even though Isabel was again pregnant. He still preferred the dangerous route down the Amazon, perhaps because he knew that La Condamine had made a successful descent of the river back in 1743. He would go alone, with Isabel to follow as soon as possible after the baby was born. He would check every bit of the way for her, prepare the missions for her coming, and would himself return as far as a ship could go up the river to meet her. He would send word just as soon as he reached the Atlantic Ocean and the colony of French Guiana. His journey across the Andes to the Oriente, then down the Bobonaza River, the Pastaza, the Marañon, the Amazon to the sea would take many months, but Isabel would hear from him as soon as possible, in a year or two. He left at the beginning of March 1749.

The baby was born in due course, a girl who was named Carmen. She seemed healthy. Now Isabel waited only for news to come from Jean so that she could make her arrangements. During this time she must have spent hours and days dreaming about everything she had read of France and Paris, where she would join Jean again for a wonderful life. She would miss Riobamba and its pleasant society, but really not too much with all the excitement of a new country.

Isabel Godin waited for news. She waited for years and years. She grew older, changing gradually from a vivid young girl (she was only twenty when Jean left) to a mature woman, then to an older woman with streaks of white in her luxurious black hair.

Eighteen years passed while Isabel Godin waited. Malicious gossipers may have suggested to her that her husband had left for France not intending to return or send for her. Perhaps he had found another woman or did not think a wife from the audiencia of Quito suitable to appear in Paris. This is not mentioned in accounts of that time and maybe there was no suspicion. Apparently there was none on Isabel's part.

It is unfortunate that no word has come down to us from Isabel directly—no journal, no letters. We have to depend on rumor and imagination. She was a famous woman of her time. When news of her adventures reached Europe she became the talk of the salons in Paris, the coffeehouses in London. There were conflicting, often fanciful, reports of her journey and her earlier life. I let my imagination wander, basing my speculations on what I did know of the place, the time, and the person.

Isabel, overjoyed to have her fourth child live and

prosper, must have spent her days caring for little Carmen, then teaching her at home, taking her to school, seeing that she had all the advantages her place in society offered. Music lessons, dancing lessons, painting lessons. She must have read to her the old stories of the Amazons and the City of Gold, explaining over and over again how, soon, her father would send for them both. No doubt she taught her Quechua as well as French and perhaps explained to her the fascinating mysteries of the quipu, the device used by the Incas to keep accounts and record events by means of knotted strings of various colors. Isabel was known to have interested herself in this, along with other Inca customs, and to have been unusually expert in its use.

Meanwhile, the years slipped by, and Carmen grew up. She was five years older than Isabel had been when she married Jean. No doubt she had suitors; perhaps she planned to marry.

Time passed relentlessly. Snows fell on the volcanoes in winter, melted in the spring to nourish the fields and fill the rivers. Hummingbirds nested on Tungurahua and their fledglings matured and flew away. Wars and threats of war came and went. These may not have interested Isabel, but they were one reason why she never heard from Jean and a principal reason why he could not get permission to ascend the Amazon to fetch her. It is hard to believe that in all that time Jean could not have corresponded with his wife, but there is no indication that he ever did. He said later that he didn't know of his daughter's birth until she was more than two years old, and that the news came not from Riobamba, but from France.

Catastrophe struck when, at the age of eighteen, Carmen died suddenly of yellow fever. Her daughter gone, Isabel had nothing to live for except the hope, now certainly faint, of seeing Jean again. She gave way to melancholy and is said by one writer to have sat at the window all day long, every day, watching for someone—Jean?—to come. Isabel's family gave her all their support. Her mother had died, but her father, the general, was still living. He was now old and Isabel's brother Antonio managed the property. Her brother José had become a monk at the Augustine monastery. Time crept on. It seemed that Isabel's life would remain fixed like a painting set in a moment of her existence. Nothing would ever change.

Then one day José burst into the house with strange news. The friars at the monastery had a series of missions, some of them on the river Amazon. These communities were a grapevine of rumors, and this one might be sheer gossip, but word had it, by way of brother this and brother that, that Isabel's husband Jean was alive, that he was waiting in Cayenne at the mouth of the Amazon. Further, the king of Portugal had sent a galliot to meet Isabel at Loreto, the highest navigable point on the river, thence to bring her down to the ocean and to a reunion with Jean.

From the details we know of her, Isabel always showed a practical turn of mind. She did not instantly rush to pack her possessions and start the trek over the Andes and down the rivers. She knew how rumors traveled, especially in the monasteries, true or false, and she could not afford to trust the monks' word with no verification, even though the news was marvelously good. She sent her "faithful servant" Joaquin across the mountains to the Amazon to check up on it. He was Isabel's most loyal retainer, a black slave brought in from the Caribbean to work in the fields where he suffered daily abuse, starvation, all sorts of cruelty until Isabel heard of his wretched existence and bought his freedom. Of all her party on the river journey, he was the one who would work the hardest to prevent the catastrophes that befell her. Joaquin set off. He appeared back in Riobamba some months later, after a hard journey through the jungle, to report. There was indeed a Portuguese galliot waiting at Loreto, as it would continue to do, until Isabel Godin des Odonais should turn up to descend the river. Jean had written her a letter, Joaquin said, but it had been passed from mission to mission and had never arrived. He was still waiting at Cayenne and longing for her to join him.

With this positive news, Isabel's preparations became frenzied. She had always been pampered and now she was forty, no longer young. Her journey, even if there were no unexpected difficulties, would be very hard. Her father worried, but he decided that it would be easier for her to go down the rivers than to spend weeks riding a mule to Guayaquil on the Pacific where she could board a ship. After all, the galliot waited, and the weeks on the Bobonaza and the Pastaza Rivers could be made tolerable if he went ahead to be sure that canoes, food, Indian rowers, shelter, were waiting for her at every stop. He left to make the arrangements. At the same time, he would let the captain of the galliot, who had already waited for months, know that his passenger was coming.

During the next month Isabel was busy selling her furniture, sorting her possessions, saying goodbye forever to her relatives and friends. However, several members of the family did not plan to remain behind. The idea of Paris had its fascination. Antonio decided he must take his nine-year-old son, Isabel's nephew, to France for schooling. The monk José saw this as an opportunity to continue from Paris to Italy to visit the Vatican.

Isabel's father sent her a letter by a traveling friar. He was on his way down the Pastaza River to Loreto where the galliot waited, and all the preparations had been made.

"My daughter," he wrote, "everything is ready. In the town of Canelos canoes are waiting and oarsmen to row them. The roads are bad. Keep the luggage you take as little as possible and take no more people than are necessary. The number of canoes and the space in them is limited."

Canoes, as built by experienced Indian river-runners, were of a fairly uniform size. The typical craft was about forty-four feet long and the width of two wide tree trunks. The rowers took their places from the bow back to the center, while the passengers and baggage occupied a small cabin under a roof of interlaced palm leaves. Light was provided to the cabin by a sort of door or window. The canoes traveled day and night, the oarsmen sleeping by turns at their places.

The fewer passengers the better, so Isabel refused the pleas of a French doctor, "Monsieur R.," as he is referred to. He had arrived from Guayaquil unheralded to ask for passage to Cayenne—her journey was evidently talked about way over on the Pacific coast. Isabel refused him—he was not likable and she suspected that he was not really a doctor—but her brothers persuaded her to take him along. His medical knowledge might come in handy on the long trip. The doctor had a servant, and Isabel's three chola maids, Rosa, Elvira, and Eloisa, would accompany her along with the faithful Joaquin. This made a total of ten travelers, more than the ordinary river canoe should be expected to handle.

We have no record of what Isabel packed for her journey but we do know that she was not used to a simple life. The writer Zuñiga describes the possessions of Pedro Vicente

Maldonado, one of Isabel's neighbors. He gives what is almost an inventory of the Maldonado home: "Curtained salons, mirrors framed in ebony and tortoiseshell, chairs from Russia, sculptures from Spain, sheets from Britain, lace-trimmed Cambray pillowslips, slippers of cloth of gold, garments of velvet and silk."

The Grandmaisons were no doubt as used to luxury as the Maldonados. Pedro Maldonado, when he made the Amazon descent with La Condamine years before, had set out with a mountain of possessions and supplies. Two big chests carried money alone. Others contained valuable objects of silver and gold. He completed his voyage without losing any of these things, which he planned to turn in for a magnificent profit in Paris. Even La Condamine, not the type to barter goods for money, carried heavy equipment, all the instruments that he had not sold in Quito at the end of the scientific work. His telescope alone was three and a half meters long, requiring to be loaded on the backs of two mules traveling in tandem.

Isabel must have spent many hours packing and unpacking, trying to travel light, as her father had advised.

Probably she packed a good supply of dresses, skirts, shawls, shoes with gold buckles, belts studded with silver, lace-trimmed underwear, embroidered parasols, lengths of the finest cloth woven from vicuña wool to make up later according to Paris fashion. We know, from later references, that she took not only clothes but such things as silver bowls as well.

All these things were loaded on mules and on the backs of Indians, along with baggage for the rest of the party. The pack train also carried food for humans and animals, blankets, and other gear. Altogether the baggage required thirty-one bearers. They were men of the high country who had never been near the jungle or set foot in a canoe. That would come later. First they must make the long journey across the towering mountain passes to the embarcation point at Canelos on the Bobonaza River. It would not be easy to cross the cordillera, especially now in the fall when rain was coming on, but once at Canelos, where her father had said there was a large settlement, arrangements could be made to obtain extra canoes for the trip on the waterways.

No mention is made by any chronicler of what this group of city people planned to wear as they journeyed down the world's most dangerous rivers. The men were not too poorly equipped with their kneebreeches and cloaks and shoes, over which they could wear heavy woolen Indian ponchos. The women's situation was different, and I am afraid we must picture Isabel setting out determinedly wearing long skirts, a straw hat, and dainty shoes. However, since she was going to be protected from all hardships and to travel in luxury, this hardly mattered.

Altogether it had taken two years for Isabel to learn of the ship that awaited her at Loreto, to check on the accuracy of the report, and to make preparations for departure from Riobamba. It was October 1, 1769, when her party finally set out.

THIRTEEN

JEAN GODIN SAID GOODBYE to Isabel and started his journey downriver to the Atlantic in March 1748, taking thirteen long months for the trip. There were no more than the usual difficulties and he arrived safely at Para, where the river emptied into the ocean, and proceeded from there along the coast to French Guiana, where he settled at Oyapok, an agricultural colony across the border from Brazil. He had left Riobamba in order to attend to urgent business in France. He departed with every assurance that he would return up the Amazon and meet his wife at Loreto as soon as she had had her baby and raised the child to an age where he or she could safely travel.

So far as we know, Jean did not go to France. He did not return up the river for Isabel. Why? We have his explanation in a letter written to La Condamine years later, in 1773:

> I arrived at Cayenne in April . . . and immediately wrote
> to M. Rouille, then minister of the Navy, intreating him to

procure me passports and recommendations to the court of Portugal, to enable me to ascend the Amazons, for the purpose of proceeding to my family, and bringing it back with me by the same channel.

Also I availed myself of the opportunity afforded by the conveyance which took my letters to forward several objects pertaining to natural history for the King's garden; among others seed of the sarsaparilla, and of the five species of butua; with these also a grammar, printed in Lima, of the language of the Incas, which I designed as a present for M. de Buffon, from whom I received no answer. . . . From M. Rouille, I learnt that His Majesty had been pleased to direct that the governor and intendant of Cayenne should both furnish me with recommendations to the government of Para.

Upon this, I wrote to you, Sir, and you were so obliging as to solicit passports for me. You moreover favoured me with a letter of recommendation from Commander La Cerda, minister of Portugal to France, addressed to the governor of Para, with a letter from M. l'Abbé de la Ville, which informed you that my passports had been expedited, and forwarded to Para. I enquired respecting them of the governor of that place, who expressed his entire ignorance of the fact. I repeated my letters to M. Rouille, who then was no longer in the ministry.

Why the preoccupation with passports? I remembered that the French Mission had only received clearance to enter Peru because they were a bona fide scientific expedition, and that this had required special permission from royalty. Ordinarily neither Spain nor Portugal allowed foreigners to enter their valuable territories in the New World. Jean's efforts were directed at procuring a French passport and permission to enter Portuguese and Spanish holdings in his journey up the Amazon. He would have had no trouble coming down the river because he was returning from an authorized expedition, and Isabel, besides the fact that she was Spanish, might have used the same reasoning when she followed her husband.

Various "papers and documents" were lost when Isabel was finally sent for by the Portuguese galliot. No doubt they were passports and transit papers for her and her family to make the journey through Portuguese Brazil to the Atlantic coast. But that's getting ahead of the story.

For Jean in Guiana, bureaucracy had run amok, made worse by distance, the wars, uncertain communications, and the fact that three nations were involved when a Frenchman traveled on the Amazon: Spain, France, and Portugal. Jean kept up his efforts.

"Since that time," he wrote to La Condamine,

I renewed my letters every year, four, five, and even six times, for the purpose of obtaining my passports, and constantly without effect. Many of my letters were lost, or intercepted during the war.

At length, hearing casually that M. le Comte d'Herouville was in the confidence of M. de Choiseul, I ventured, in 1765 [he had been writing letters for fifteen years!] to write to the former of these noblemen entreating him to intercede with the Duc de Choiseul for the transmission of my passports.

To the kindness of this nobleman alone can I attribute the success that followed this step; for, the tenth month from the date of my letter . . . I saw a decked galliot arrive at Cayenne, equipped at Para by order of the King of Portugal, manned with thirty oars, and commanded by a captain of the garrison of Para, instructed to bring me to Para, thence transport me up the river as high as the first Spanish settlement, to wait there until I returned with my

family, and ultimately reconduct me to Cayenne, all at
the special charge of His Most Faithful Majesty, a liberal-
ity truly royal, and such as is little common among
sovereigns.

Jean, while writing letters and waiting for answers, was
occupied, during the endless years of delay, in the usual
activities of a settler in Guiana. He went into agriculture and
commercial fishing and became prominent in the small
colony, conferring with the governor and advising him on
community projects. So the time passed in day by day
activities as month followed month and the years crept by.

⚜

Guiana had a briefer history of European contact than Quito.
The first foreigners reached there in 1604, led by Daniel de
La Ravadière, seeking El Dorado. Sir Walter Raleigh landed
there later and described a "region of people whose heads
appear not above their shoulders . . . they are reported to
have their eyes in their shoulders and . . . mouths in the
middle of their breasts, and that a long train of hair groweth
backward between their shoulders." Physical anomalies
fascinated readers of armchair travel in those days.

As time went on, several French maritime companies tried
to settle colonists in Cayenne without success. In 1686 an
expedition under the privateer Jean Baptiste Ducasse was
decimated by the army of Dutch Guiana, and no Frenchman
arrived for the next fifteen years. Then, between 1700 and
1763, the family of Orvilliers held the nominal governorship
of the colony; and the Duc de Choiseul sent colonists, who
died of fever. But small groups continued to arrive and some

134

of them lived and prospered. Cayenne was the capital, but Oyapok, where Jean Godin settled, became prosperous.

French Guiana was small, with a coastline two hundred miles long. To the north the Atlantic rolled in; to the south two hundred and fifty miles inland through snake-infested jungle, the Tumac Humac Mountains jutted upward. On the east the Oyapok River formed the border with Brazil. The town of Oyapok, at the river's mouth, dominated by Fort Louis, was a ramshackle village where Indians built their houses in trees to escape the floods and Frenchmen, living away from the riverbanks, owned plantations of sugar, coffee, and coconuts, with a plentiful supply of slaves to do the hard work. Immigration, for a Frenchman, was easy, and the region was being developed in an orderly fashion. Crops were raised on a coastal strip twenty miles wide, in rich alluvial soil, while inland, past mangrove swamps, the forest began, trackless, endless.

La Condamine had visited Guiana after his own voyage down the Amazon some years before. He arrived in Cayenne in February 1744 and stayed five months, keeping busy as usual. He performed experiments on the speed of sound, studied the sea cow, made a map of the territory, and planted seeds of quinine he had brought from Peru, assisted in these endeavors by his friend Maldonado until they both sailed off to Europe in 1745.

La Condamine was not forgotten; a mountain in the commune of Kourou was named for him. Today, Kourou boasts a French satellite ground station, something La Condamine could not have imagined.

Guiana was known as the "Wild Coast." In the sea lived giant whales, while huge turtles floated lazily along the shore. On land, the visitor was intoxicated by the fragrance of lemons, limes, oranges, and all kinds of exotic flowers.

Along the shore mangroves and palms grew in profusion, and back from the coast were magnificent hardwood forests. Fields of sugarcane covered the open plains. Even the sugar was fragrant; it smelled like violets.

Settlers lived in houses with big rooms and high windows for coolness, the masters' homes built separately from the servants' cabins. The river Oyapok was full of fish; in the forest, besides monkeys and tapirs, were deer and wild cattle. Anyone who pretended to fashionable living had two servants assigned for hunting only, and two others as fishermen. There were mosquitoes and sandflies, and occasional tropical storms. Settlers, if they survived, became resistant to fever, suffering, according to reports, more often from jaundice and insomnia.

Jean says nothing in his long letter to La Condamine about his life in Oyapok, except for his efforts to send for Isabel. Perhaps La Condamine already knew of his projects, but our questions remain unanswered. Did Jean Godin take another wife or mistress from among the women of this tropical land? That would not be surprising; he spent twenty years there, a third of his lifetime. But if he did, he never forgot Isabel. She became an obsession, a distant dream of an idyllic life on the great estate in the altiplano with its snowcapped, steaming volcanoes and its society of cultivated Spaniards; those years of his youth when he studied Quechua with a beautiful child, married her, and enjoyed a perfect existence.

Jean Godin's letter to La Condamine raises an array of other questions. What happened to the many unanswered letters over all those years? There was no regular mail service, but messages and letters usually did arrive eventually. Why didn't Jean write some of those letters to his wife, sending them upriver with traveling friars, or around to

Cartagena, or even by way of France and back again? He had left Riobamba to take care of urgent business in France, yet he did not actually make a journey there until 1773, almost twenty-five years after his father's death, when the estate must have been long settled. Why not? Why, when the galliot was finally dispatched, was it ordered by the king of Portugal himself? Was Jean Godin so important, when he was finally noticed at all, as to receive the attention of royalty?

Whatever the answers to these questions, the galliot did arrive at Cayenne and Jean went to meet it. "We left Cayenne at the close of November 1765," he writes to La Condamine, "in order to take in property belonging to me at the fort of Oyapok, where I resided. Here I fell sick, and even dangerously so. M. de Rebello, the captain, a knight of the order of Christ, was so complaisant as to wait for me six weeks; finding at length that I still continued too ill to venture on the voyage . . . I besought him to continue his route, and that he would permit me to put someone on board, to whom I might entrust my letters, and who might fill my place in taking care of my family on its return."

Jean selected a longtime friend, Tristan, to go up the river on the Portuguese ship and deliver all the necessary documents and letters that would allow Isabel to return with him to Guiana. Tristan, however, failed in his mission. He gave the papers to a friar who gave them to another, and they never did reach Riobamba. He himself went into the trading business along the river and showed no concern for Isabel or for his friend, Jean Godin.

Jean continues: "Spite, however, of his bad conduct, a vague rumor reached the ears of Madame Godin, not only of letters addressed to her being on their way in the custody of a Jesuit, but also, that in the uppermost missions of Portugal a vessel equipped by his most Faithful Majesty had arrived to transport her to Cayenne. . . . With respect to the arrival of the vessel, opinions differed, some giving credit to, while others disputed the fact . . ."

So we come full circle to Isabel in Riobamba, hearing rumors, dispatching Joaquin, waiting the many months for his return, then embarking on her long journey.

Still, a number of questions spring to mind. I wonder what was the serious illness that prevented Jean from boarding the Portuguese vessel and making the upriver trip. Six weeks was a long time to be ill in those days; patients recovered naturally or died. I notice, too, that Jean never did go up the Amazon, then or later. The reason, gleaned from other sources, was one that he could not risk putting in a letter to La Condamine, because it might come into the wrong hands.

When years had passed with no answer to his requests for passports and permission to bring Isabel down to Guiana, Jean wrote a letter that was bound to attract attention. He sent the Duc de Choiseul a complete plan for a French takeover of part of the Amazon controlled by the Portuguese. He was able to outline details of how a French fleet could operate from Guiana, capturing the salient points on the Amazon so that France, not Portugal, would control the route to all the southern seas. He sent this off, as usual, by a traveling friar.

There was one thing wrong with the proposal: it never reached the Duc de Choiseul but disappeared en route. Jean Godin, on learning this, was seized with terror. The Portuguese, he felt sure, were in possession of the letter, waiting only for an opportunity to take him prisoner.

Before the galliot arrived Jean had built a ship himself, intending to ascend the Amazon on it. He set out, but had not even reached the mouth of the river when he returned, possessed with the idea that the Portuguese were lying in wait. He stayed in Guiana, and when the galliot arrived at Cayenne it meant to him that the Portuguese were closing in. He did board the ship, however, and proceeded to Oyapok, where he claimed to have business to take care of. Here he feigned all sorts of delays, hoping the captain would give up and leave.

Finally Jean invented, or really suffered, an illness, perhaps sickness of apprehension. He enlisted Tristan to go upriver in his place and the vessel sailed.

No attempt was ever made against Jean. The ship was a true rescue vessel sent for Isabel Godin, but Jean never recovered his sanity completely; he suspected Portuguese treachery at every turn. No trace was ever found of his letter with its plan to take over the Amazon—lost, apparently, in the mail.

FOURTEEN

FOR ISABEL, THE DEPARTURE from Riobamba must have been a solemn moment. She was leaving, undoubtedly forever, the city where she had spent all her life, in which she had been a lively girl, a devoted wife, and a sad woman alone, waiting and hoping.

I have often thought how fortunate it was that Jean Godin was a talented writer. Most of what we know of his wife's journey we learn from his long letter to La Condamine written when he and Isabel finally arrived in France. For the rest, much can be deduced from what we know of eighteenth-century life in colonial Peru and the experiences of other travelers in the vast expanses of the Amazon basin.

The party set out on muleback in single file, over the rough trail, with the Indian bearers slogging along behind on foot. The road wound for several miles over the plain, gradually gaining altitude. The yellow broom, which blossomed at this season, gave way to coarse brown ichu grass. As they mounted the slopes of Tungurahua Volcano there were no more trees, no flowers. Falcons circled overhead and the campanero bird gave out his lonely bell-like cry.

This was Isabel's first opportunity for travel, and what exciting travel it would be. After this beginning stretch, surely the most arduous of the journey, she would enjoy a reasonably comfortable ride in a canoe down thousands of miles of rivers. There would be missions to stop at, new country to see, and always the expectation of finding her husband Jean. No doubt shelters had been prepared along the route by Indians on the instructions of General Grandmaison, where the large party must have camped each night on the slopes of the volcano, cooking whatever they carried with them or what the Indians had provided. They probably had some live animals along for provisions at the start of the journey, a fat pig perhaps, a dozen chickens. In three days of hard travel they reached Baños, then, as now, a pleasant watering spot. Here they rested and prepared for the week's march down to the Oriente and Canelos. The road from here on was too rough and narrow for mules. The trail went back and forth across streams and waterfalls, using swinging bridges of vines where pack animals could not venture. The track would be negotiated on foot by everyone except Isabel. Her father, when he passed through Baños, had left her a conveyance of his own design, a sort of sedan chair to be carried by Indians, much like the chariot of the early Inca emperors. It was roomy, with a palm-leaf roof.

The days from Baños to Canelos were a nightmare of rain, mud, dangerous river crossings. Surely the rest of their passage would be almost enjoyable, or at least interesting, as Isabel and her companions floated swiftly and comfortably down the waterways—the Bobonaza to the Pastaza to the Marañon to the Amazon itself. From Loreto, where they would join Isabel's father, they would have luxurious accommodations in the Portuguese galliot along the magnificent Amazon to the sea. How many days of travel? Not days, months. In a week, when they reached Canelos, they could stay a night or two at the mission, transferring their goods to the waiting canoes, hiring boatmen, sorting their possessions, and adding fresh food to their supplies.

Meanwhile the trail was rough, it poured rain, and the line of forty-one people snaked slowly along. They continued to follow the flank of the volcano, the track making loops and turns as it passed around cliffs and through gullies. The bridges over rapids swung terrifyingly under the weight of the travelers. On the fourth day from Baños they crossed the last pass from which they would make the final descent to the Oriente. There was no sign yet of the green jungle. The slopes of Tungurahua still rose beside them, forbidding, brown, and lonely.

They now descended, still following a rough trail, to country wholly different from the high plains. Monkeys swung in trees, parrots screeched, a forest of green vines and undergrowth almost choked the trail. Hordes of mosquitoes attacked the travelers. Now the river Bobonaza ran beside the trail, dark and rapid, forcing its way past submerged trees and rocks. The stream was narrow, some two hundred feet wide, but deep. In its depths might lurk man-eating fish, electric eels. What seemed to be a rough log resting against the bank might just as well be an alligator.

Tall trees arched over the river, laced together with vines that sprang from the bank. The sky was cut off under a green canopy, and there was no view ahead.

Flights of parrots burst from the trees above the line of travelers, their brilliant colors flashing. Across the river the band of monkeys howled. A big green lizard slithered across the trail in front of Isabel's sedan chair. Two tapirs could be heard whistling to each other in the bushes, and a giant otter leaped into the water in a graceful dive and disappeared downstream. The air was so humid that the travelers seemed to be breathing steam, not air.

As the commotion caused by human beings died down, the jungle became silent, a menacing silence.

They continued to trudge along the trail until at last they neared the mission town of Canelos. There they expected to find friendly people waiting for them, alerted by General Grandmaison to assist his daughter's party. They would soon meet the resident missionary, and the band of mission Indians who would start them on the long canoe voyage downriver.

The line of walkers quickened their pace; the path was easier here than it had been on the flanks of the volcano. The Indians carrying Isabel's chair stopped to wipe their faces and chew their coca. They exchanged words with their leader and four others took their places.

At midafternoon the party suddenly halted. An Indian near the head of the line cried out. He seemed to be shouting "Fire!" but perhaps it was merely a cry of excitement. The path widened here and the rest of the party crowded up to look around. A column of smoke rose over the dense forest to dissipate in the sky. There was a heavy acrid smell of burning. Canelos must be no more than a few minutes away.

The pace quickened again. The Indians murmured and took up a sort of trot. The column of smoke was nearer now, too big for a cooking fire.

Abruptly the party emerged into a large clearing beside the river. The smoke rose ahead of them straight into the still air. There were houses in the clearing, a number of them, a sizable settlement, but there were no human beings in sight. The travelers shouted, but only a faint echo came back.

The big mission building burned rapidly, one wing of it already consumed. Whatever had happened here, the town of Canelos, which they had journeyed so many days to reach, was no longer a town. It was abandoned, ready to sink back into the all-embracing ravenous jungle.

They discovered two Indians hiding in the woods, fearing to return to an infected town. The town had been struck by smallpox, many had died there, and the rest had left. The fire had been started to "clear the air" in the stricken village. There were no canoes, for the Indians had fled in them, and there were no oarsmen. To make things worse, the thirty-one Indians who had come with the travelers from Riobamba deserted during the night and disappeared into the jungle. They were afraid of illness or, possibly, were unwilling to embark in a canoe, a vessel they had never seen before, to travel on a strange river through a terrifying jungle.

The party, which now numbered ten, were in a serious predicament, brought on perhaps by the general's efforts to be sure that Isabel had a trouble-free journey. He had passed through a month before, and one of his Indian bearers had come down with the disease and started the epidemic that quickly obliterated the town.

"What under such circumstances was to be done?" Jean wrote in his letter to La Condamine. "Had my wife been able to return, yet the desire of reaching the vessel awaiting her, together with her anxiety to rejoin a husband from whom she had been parted twenty years, were incentives powerful enough to make her, in the peculiar circumstances in which she was placed, brave even greater obstacles."

So Isabel found herself stranded in a deserted town that was burning to purify the air according to Indian belief, with no canoes in sight since the fleeing natives had taken them, and with her own natives defected. Impossible to return through the mountains if she had wanted to, apparently impossible to proceed.

It is evident throughout this story that Isabel was the leader of the expedition. This seems strange for a time when women did not lead expeditions or take command, officially, of anything. It tells us something of her determined character. Her two brothers were along, but they made no decisions. Her father had written his instructions to her, as head of the family, not to Antonio or José. Now it was up to her to find a way out of this impasse.

Isabel never doubted that the party should proceed. If some of the group wanted to go back, they were overruled. Besides, how could they go back without their Indian guides who had vanished into the forest?

She turned to the two Indians who were all that remained of Canelos's population, and bargained with them for assistance. They had no boat but agreed, if Isabel paid them a large sum in advance, to build a canoe big enough for the whole party. They would then pilot them to Andoas, a mission town about twelve days' journey downriver. Against her better judgment, Isabel paid them in advance, knowing that they had the group entirely in their power. The Indians quickly set about constructing a canoe and completed the work in a week. No doubt it was built according to traditional river design, an open vessel about forty feet long, fashioned from the hollowed-out trunks of enormous trees, with a small palm-leaf shelter near the stern. It was just large enough to accommodate the ten travelers plus the two Indian boatmen.

A great deal of the baggage must have been abandoned in Canelos. The burdens of thirty-one Indians would never fit in one canoe. Yet, from later notes, we know that Isabel did load aboard such items as silver bowls, snuff boxes, skirts of taffeta and velvet, rosaries of gold, and earrings set with emeralds. I think some of these possessions were Isabel's precaution against possible money problems in the future—they would bring a big price in Paris. Like many very rich people, she evidently worried about finances. The skirts? I find it touching that Isabel still cared about fashionable dress even after days of rugged travel in the mountains and with the prospect of months on the great rivers. But then, she had no suspicion of the terrible events to come.

Food was essential, enough to meet the needs of a dozen people for many days. Staple provisions probably included chuño, the freeze-dried potatoes known for centuries to the Incas; charqui, dried meat of llama, sheep, or pig (from which the modern word jerky is descended) paiche or pirarucu, a huge fish of the Amazon basin, eaten fresh or dried, which the river Indians would have favored; and from Riobamba dried corn, beans, biscuits. The men of the party would provide fresh food by hunting the wild turkeys, iguanas, and partridge along the river, while the Indians caught fresh fish or killed river turtles. There were chirimoyas ripe at this season on the fruit trees, wild grapes, and birds' eggs. That would be an adequate larder against the possibility of starvation.

The Indian oarsmen would be expected to build each evening a ramada on the bank of the river, a shelter of branches that they knew how to put up in a very short time, as La Condamine had remarked.

As they climbed aboard the newly built canoe and headed downstream, the passengers must, in spite of the setbacks, have looked with interest at the river and the jungle they were passing. That far upstream, the Bobonaza was still narrow, a dark rushing torrent of water swirling among boulders, splashing around fallen branches, keeping up a low roaring sound. The two Indians paddled with the confidence of experienced rowers.

Jean Godin's letter to La Condamine describing his wife's journey records events meticulously but, since both men knew the Amazon basin well, it does not elaborate on the jungle background. I was anxious to see the forest as Isabel saw it. Fortunately there are few areas of the world that have been better described than this one.

Parts of the jungle are like a great cathedral of lofty arching trees whose trunks rise straight up for sixty or seventy feet before branches arch out to form a canopy. In such areas there is little underbrush, just a thin growth of ferns and dwarf palms. There are dim shady vistas of a hundred feet or more where deer may run or jaguars prowl. The shadowy naves of this cathedral disappear in a green ceiling far overhead. Vines rise through the branches, clutching them in a stranglehold. The jungle here is vast, mysterious. It dwarfs a human being.

Other parts of the jungle are aptly described as "green hell." This is the aspect I usually think of, where a leaf-green curtain covers everything, and its depth can only be penetrated with the help of a machete. In the cathedral what one sees is impressive; in the wet leafy jungle what one does not see is terrifying. There are countless inhabitants of this jungle: fire ants, crickets, cicadas, frogs in the marshes, mosquitoes in the air. Big bright-hued butterflies flutter about; howler monkeys swing from branch to branch; hundreds of species of insects, beetles, caterpillars, and bees share the jungle. Near the river otters chatter and families of large ratlike capybaras bark. Turtles and alligators doze on the riverbank. There are snakes, from venomous fer-de-lances to thirty-foot anacondas, but they are not as numerous as usually believed. The staccato rapping sound may be a woodpecker striking a tree trunk; the whistle may be a tapir calling its mate. The sounds are innumerable, but the jungle is also sometimes silent, a silence more intense than the mere absence of sound.

For two days Isabel and her party descended the river in the canoe with the two Indians paddling. I imagine that she enjoyed those days. She had successfully solved the quandary of how to proceed. Perhaps she congratulated herself a bit. After all, if she had not learned Quechua during those years at home, she would not have been able to bargain with the oarsmen. And here she was, finally embarked on the voyage she had dreamed of, seeing a multitude of fascinating sights: the flight of hundreds of cobalt-blue butterflies settling on the riverbank in a flurry of quivering wings. Or a flock of macaws lighting to peck at a patch of clay. The birds were a moving rainbow, their bodies bright red, their wings and tails blue and yellow, their faces white.

In the evening the oarsmen choose a camping spot, some open patch a little way from the riverbank. They tie the canoe securely to overhanging tree branches and everyone goes ashore while the Indians hastily put up a flimsy shelter of palm branches and sticks, enough to keep away rain. They build a fire, making it a little larger than necessary for cooking so as to frighten away any predators wandering in the night. Isabel would have no need to busy herself with any of these tasks, and the three maidservants would take care of the cooking—fresh fish, perhaps, caught by Antonio, who fancied himself skilled with a fishing rod, and some of the dried corn boiled up with a slice of charqui into a tasty soup, a swallow or two of the French brandy they had brought along, a bunch of wild grapes, and a slice of cheese.

Jean's letter says little about Isabel's nine-year-old

nephew, Antonio's son. He doesn't even tell us his name, but I call the child Luis and I picture him as Isabel's special concern. She must have kept him reassured in the strangeness of the jungle, staying close to him in the canoe and thinking up interesting games to play in the ramada as supper simmers in a pot hung on a crane over the bonfire.

The party might hope for a favorable voyage under the protection of a watchful God. José is a monk, used to the rigorous life of the monastery. No doubt he has prayers to say that reassure the travelers in their wild surroundings.

All goes well for two days on the river. Andoas must now be only ten days away. A long, wearisome ten days, for now the wonders of the jungle have begun to pall. Isabel's only preoccupation is to get it over with, to continue on her way to the final wonderful meeting with Jean. She takes a stick of dead wood and makes a little notch in it with a kitchen knife. She makes another. This will cover the two days so far on the river and she will keep on marking off the days, the weeks, the months until the journey is over.

Jean Godin describes what happened next: "After navigating the river two days, the pilots absconded; the unfortunate party embarked without anyone to steer the boat, but passed the day without accident."

Here Isabel may have reproached herself. She should not have paid the Indians ahead of time. Of course she knew that, but what else could she have done? The journey suddenly loomed ahead, not just wearisome, but dangerous. No one among the passengers had ever managed a canoe. There were rapids to negotiate, huge floating logs and hidden rocks to avoid. There was no discussion of this problem for there was no choice. Joaquin, the black slave, and Isabel's brother Antonio picked up the oars, the others crowded aboard, and they proceeded partly rowing, partly drifting down the current.

The next day at noon they saw a canoe in a small port adjoining a leafbuilt hut. They beached their own canoe and Isabel, accompanied by Antonio, went ashore. In the hut they found a native recovering from illness. Here Isabel, the leader of the expedition, was the one to persuade the Indian, using words of Quechua, the lingua franca of all that area, to take charge of the canoe and guide them to Andoas. After this, Isabel was able to mark off three days on her stick without incident. In the evenings the men of the party helped the Indian to put up a shelter; he was too weak to accomplish it by himself.

Jean continues: "On the third day of his voyage, while stooping over to recover the hat of Monsieur K., which had fallen into the water, the poor man fell overboard and, not having sufficient strength to reach the shore, was drowned. Behold the canoe, again without a steersman, abandoned to individuals perfectly ignorant of managing it . . . "

Who was this Monsieur K.? It was the custom, in Jean Godin's time, to refer to people by their initials, especially if the remarks to be made about them were uncomplimentary. I remember that Isabel had accepted the French doctor with reluctance. She didn't like him; she suspected he was not even a doctor. It seems likely that he was the passenger who let his hat fall into the water and then expected the oarsman to retrieve it.

In any case the men of the party had to continue handling the canoe, and this time they were not so lucky. Suddenly the current caught it, swirled it around, and it capsized, fortunately close to the shore. Everyone was able to climb the bank and the canoe was righted without much damage to the cargo.

The upset did more than alarm the travelers. It destroyed their confidence entirely. No one wanted to step aboard the canoe and continue downstream and anyway, it was late in the day. They stayed ashore and built themselves a hut. After helping the oarsman for the last three days, they now had some idea how to construct it so that it gave at least makeshift protection. That night, Isabel, perhaps with small Luis sleeping beside her, must have thought about the situation with fear and discouragement. It seemed as though, whenever things seemed to be going well, some incident occurred and the group were back in their dilemma again. At least, she may have thought, we are together, Antonio, José, little Luis, the girls, the doctor and his servant—we are all in the same situation, all together. That is some support. It would be terrible to be here in the jungle alone. There was no reason to fear solitude, so she surely did not dwell on this. Ten people is a big group, in some ways too big. She slept.

The jungle found its true voice in the blackness of the night. Branches creaked, monkeys howled, heavy footsteps padded around the shelter. Mosquitoes descended in swarms. Yellow eyes shone in the dark. A small animal screamed. Something splashed into the water close by the hut. Rain dripped like a leaky faucet from the tree branches. The travelers slept fitfully, tossing in fever or chills, for now some of them were stricken with "tertian fever," malaria. They now suffered nightmares worse than reality.

In the morning the doctor, here referred to as "Monsieur R.," approached Isabel with a proposal. He and his servant would take the canoe down the river to Andoas, now only five or six days' journey away. There he would round up a rescue party, and within a fortnight a canoe should be forwarded to them with a proper complement of natives.

Isabel viewed this plan with suspicion, but again, there was no alternative. She wanted to send either Antonio or José to keep an eye on the doctor, but neither of them, after their frightening experience when the canoe capsized, was willing to venture downriver in the canoe. She did insist that Joaquin replace the doctor's servant, explaining that he was the only one of the group who had been this way before. She did not trust the doctor but she knew that the black slave was her devoted servant. She was not reassured when the doctor insisted on taking some of her possessions to be delivered, he said, to her father, thus lightening the baggage when the rescue team arrived. He was careful to take everything of his own and when the canoe had disappeared around the bend of the river, she realized that he had taken her box of jewelry. Surely that would not have overburdened a canoe.

Time now passed, day by day, as the eight remaining travelers waited in the shelter, watching the river, perhaps walking to the bend in the stream so that they could spot a canoe as soon as it approached.

Their life on the riverbank was surely grim. Food was running short and all the party except Isabel suffered from malaria. They alternated between shaking chills and burning fever and gradually their strength diminished until they were barely able to build a fire or dangle a fishing line in the water.

During this time Isabel must have thought often of Jean's journey over this same route twenty years before. She had never heard any details, but he too must have had difficulties, long periods when the future looked black and he wished that he had never left Riobamba. No, she told herself reasonably, La Condamine had gone down the rivers successfully, so had Pedro Maldonado, and no doubt so had Jean Godin. Her troubles stemmed from just one piece of bad luck—that the town of Canelos had been decimated by illness and there were no guides to take her party down the river to Andoas.

"The fortnight expired," Jean Godin wrote, "and even five and twenty days, when, giving over all hopes, they constructed a raft on which they ventured themselves. The raft, badly framed, struck against a branch of a sunken tree, and overset, all their effects perishing in the waves, and the whole party being plunged into the water. Thanks to the little breadth of the river at this place no one was drowned, Madame Godin being happily saved, after twice sinking, by her brothers."

As usual, Jean gave the facts but elaborated on them very little. As he explained to La Condamine at the beginning of his letter, it had been difficult to persuade Isabel to speak of her tragic voyage, or to give him more than the bare outline, and he himself wished only to forget it.

I can picture, however, the day when Isabel, as leader of her party, finally admitted to herself and to the others that the rescue canoe was not coming. Almost a month had passed, enough time to return even against the current. It seemed probable that the doctor and Joaquin had not made it to Andoas. They could have been wrecked and drowned in some rapids. They could have been killed by hostile Indians. They could have died of malaria, or been attacked by wild beasts.

There was no hope of seeing them round the bend in a big well-stocked canoe paddled by expert oarsmen. Isabel, always practical, always looking for a way out of each impasse, persuaded her brothers to build a raft. They must have made this of balsa wood, lightweight, easy to haul to the stream, even for men weakened by illness. They still had some tools, a machete no doubt, a hatchet, a saw, a hammer. They fastened the balsa logs together with vines and in a couple of days the raft was done. It would hold all of them—now eight people—what remained of their provisions, and some of their property.

It was an amateur job, unsteady even before the passengers got aboard. Antonio and José, who had been afraid to embark in a canoe, were now so desperate that they climbed on the raft without complaint. It was unsteady, but by moving to one side the passengers kept it level. In smooth water it would serve. They pushed off, leaving the miserable shelter where they had spent endless days and nights. No one looked back.

For a while everything went well, the raft drifted easily along in the current. It was buoyant since it was made of balsa, a wood lighter than cork, and the vines that lashed the logs together were resilient, giving easily in the waves. They might have made it downriver except for human error. Someone—Antonio perhaps—steering the raft, failed to see the branch of a sunken tree. The raft struck it and overturned. Everything was lost. The baggage was catapulted overboard and sank; the gun, the machete, the hammer sank instantly; the bundles of clothes floated a moment, then vanished; the few remaining hampers of food disappeared to the river bottom.

As this happened, all the passengers plunged into the water. The river was narrow at this point and one after another they crawled ashore. Only Isabel still struggled in the river. I suppose she must have been dressed as usual in the garments of a lady, with a skirt to her ankles. Trying to swim in that would be like swimming in a shroud. Antonio and José leaped into the water again and swam toward her. They saw her sink. She came up gasping and sank again. Once more she struggled to the surface and her brothers grasped her, one holding each arm, and dragged her to the shore. Jean, in his account, gives no details of her condition, saying merely that she was "happily saved." Up to this point she seems to have been optimistic, planning a way out of each difficulty. Now she may have lost her confidence. It seemed as though some malign fate worked against her and her party. She does not appear to have been particularly religious but no doubt José prayed for guidance. From now on she depended on the advice of all her companions, taking a vote as to each move. Jean writes:

"Placed now in a situation still more distressing than before, they collectively resolved on tracing the course of the river along its banks. How difficult of effect this enterprise, you, Sir [La Condamine], are well aware, who know how thickly the banks of the river are beset with trees, underwood, herbage and lianas, and that it is often necessary to cut one's way. They returned to their hut, took what provisions they had left behind, and began their journey."

Evidently they had not gone far down the river on the raft if they were able to return to the shelter and pick up some supplies. They must by this time have been in dreadful condition, their clothes soaked and ruined, their shoes worn-out, their arms and legs scratched and bitten by insects. Altogether they had been, from the time they left Riobamba on October 1 until they lost the raft, probably sometime near the middle of December, more than two months on their journey.

No one kept a journal of their travels and the reader of Jean Godin's account can only imagine the details. Writers since Isabel's time have often embroidered the story of her adventures for an eager audience. I think her misfortunes are enough; they don't need elaboration, but I like to imagine the daily life of the travelers as they proceeded over the Andes, down to the Oriente, and along the Bobonaza River.

I would like to know what they ate, how they dressed, what they talked about. Did the servant girls do some laundry in the river during those weeks they waited for help? Did feuds develop among the members of the group in their difficult circumstances? Did some members of the party give way to despair while others, including Isabel, resolutely kept up their courage?

Whatever their condition when they started to follow the river on foot, it could only have got worse. Going along the bank of the Bobonaza while it led them in the right direction was hideously rough going. They had to cut their way much of the time, but they had no machete left, only a knife. They had to climb through underbrush and over fallen trees. They had to battle clinging vines and bushes set with thorns. Meanwhile, following the bank, they had to follow the river's meanderings. This greatly lengthened their way and they all agreed—I think Isabel did not make the decision here—to leave the Bobonaza and strike overland. Away from the river there would be less underbrush, more enormous trees through which the walking would be comparatively easy. They would continue in the general direction of Andoas, a few days' hike away. Jean makes no statement as to how many days Isabel and her party walked, first along the riverbank and then through the trackless jungle. Certainly she would not have kept her notched stick to count the time; no doubt it drifted downstream when she went overboard from the canoe. There is no answer to questions about the details of the journey. How about the small boy—did someone carry him when the going became too rough? Did the group walk all day through the forest or did they sometimes collapse in despair, suffering as they were with chills and violent fevers? They subsisted on a few seeds, a bit of wild fruit, and the palm cabbage. They must have slept at night on the bare ground, fearing reptiles and wild beasts. Did they speak to each other or did they plod on stolidly without the will or strength to talk?

After they left the river, thirst was added to their other sufferings. No other streams appeared; there was no rain. Finally, the last blow of all, they lost their way. They disagreed on the direction of Andoas and staggered along at random through the vast monotonous jungle. It was not long before they gave up. Oppressed with hunger and thirst, with fever and weakness, they simply seated themselves on the ground and waited the approach of death. They were now overcome by "terror of the jungle," espanto de la selva. One by one, they died.

Isabel, stupefied, delirious, tormented with choking thirst, stretched herself on the ground by the corpses of her brothers and other companions. She remained in a stupor for a couple of days, or so she thought later. She waited to die, but instead she survived and at length felt her resolution and strength return. She suffered the horror of coming back to consciousness and finding herself in a scene from the charnel house. In the tropical jungle the bodies had already started to decompose, the vultures had come and the flies hung heavy. She was dressed now only in rags and her shoes were gone. She never would discuss these moments in detail, but she had a choice, as she always seemed to have: either to give up and die here as soon as possible, or to make a desperate effort to survive. Knowing what we do of her personality, it is not surprising that she chose the latter.

She could not walk through the forest barefoot so, Jean tells us in his letter, "she cut the shoes off her brother's feet and fastened the soles on her own."

Then she started to make her way all alone, at random, through the trackless wilderness.

FIFTEEN

Mexico, Spring 1992

AS I TRIED TO reconstruct the story of Isabel's desperate wanderings in the jungle, I remembered Monsieur Lemaire's lecture, the one I had happened on in the archives. He describes his first encounter with the history of his legendary great-aunt Isabel:

> In my early childhood my older brother and I went to spend two weeks of our vacation at Nevers, where our Aunt Emma lived. She was a very old lady, born in 1844, the great-grandniece of Isabel Godin.
>
> Everything was very solemn at Aunt Emma's; there seemed to be a certain atmosphere of royalty. My brother and I were fascinated by the portrait of a beautiful woman, which hung on the wall in her room near her bed.
>
> "That is the portrait of Aunt Godin," she told us, and she recounted the story as it had been told her by her mother, who had it from her father, who had in his turn heard it from his own father, Isabel's nephew.

Then Aunt Emma took out of her closet a pair of sandals, completely out of shape and flattened, made of cloth and a kind of raffia, gray and dusty looking. "These are the sandals Aunt Godin wore when she walked through the virgin forest," she told us. She took a small battered-looking notebook from a drawer, and explained that it contained notes that Aunt Godin had made during her voyage down the Amazon.

How I wish that I could see those sandals and read that notebook! Unfortunately, they have recently disappeared, either concealed or destroyed by a relative of Monsieur Lemaire, due to a family feud.

And what about the sandals? According to all accounts, Isabel cut the soles from her brother's shoes in order to make herself something to protect her feet as she trudged through the forest with its underbrush, its rocks and thorns and sticks. How could she make sandals out of shoe soles? I picture her tying the flat soles to her feet with lengths of vine, or perhaps with strips of cloth torn from her dress. In view of Monsieur Lemaire's description of the sandals he saw, either she was able to cut more than the soles from her brother's shoes or, perhaps, she managed to remove his sandals entirely—another small detail with no answer.

Jean Godin in his letter to La Condamine, went on with the story:

"It was about the period between the 25th and 30th of December, 1769, that this unfortunate party perished in this miserable manner; the date I gather by what I learn from the only survivor, who related that it was nine days after she quitted the scene . . . before she reached the banks of the Bobonaza. . . . How a female so delicately educated and in such a state of want and exhaustion, could support her distress, though but half the time, appears most wonderful. . . . The remembrance of the shocking spectacle she witnessed, the horror incident on her solitude and the darkness of night in a desert, the perpetual apprehension of death, which every instant served but to augment, had such effect on her spirits as to cause her hair to turn grey."

However she may have made those sandals from Antonio's shoes, they did protect her feet so that she could wander, slowly and uncertainly, through the jungle, which here I imagine was a vast park of trees two hundred feet high, with branches interlacing overhead and vines crowding for space in the canopy. There would have been dead trees and fallen branches to clamber over, bushes and jagged outcroppings of rock to crawl around. There would have been dim, ominous alleyways to follow between the trees with Isabel ever on the lookout, fearful of serpents, alarmed by strange rustlings in the underbrush.

She was alone and completely lost. Worst of all she was dying of thirst. On the second day she found water, a place on the jungle floor where some recent rain had left puddles. She scooped it up and drank. And on the next day, as she wandered aimlessly, she came on some wild fruit and a bird's nest with fresh eggs. What the bird was she did not know, it may have been a species of partridge. Now, however, although she was starving, she found she could hardly swallow, her throat was so parched and constricted. With much effort she was able to eat the eggs and fruit and, in the days that followed, she found just enough food, fruit and the edible leaves of some palm cabbage, to survive.

The jungle is alive with tiny voracious insects. Isabel must have suffered excruciatingly from mosquitoes. I don't know how much of her clothing was left after days of battling the jungle. At night how could she lie down with the thought of fire-eating ants, poison caterpillars, scorpions, or reptiles under the bushes? No doubt she simply collapsed from time to time, never even knowing day from night in the deep shadows of the forest. Perhaps she tore a strip of cloth from what remained of her dress and used it to cover her face from the mosquitoes.

Monkeys howled, parrots screeched. There were strange cries and outlandish grunts from whatever animals lived in the bushes or the trees. No doubt animals who had never seen a human being observed this one, a bundle of rags and flesh, slowly making her way through the forest. Once she caught hold of a bush to steady herself and a thorn pierced her left hand between the thumb and forefinger and lodged in the joint. She was not able to pull it out and the pain of it added one more discomfort to her sufferings.

Isabel was never willing to describe the horrors of her nine days in the jungle, even to Jean, so we can only imagine them. While some of those who knew her later in France felt that she had recovered emotionally, others observed that she had a pronounced facial tic that appeared when any mention was made of the jungle.

During her nine days of walking, Isabel may have described a circle. At any rate, she providentially returned to the Bobonaza. She emerged on the bank of the river at daybreak and heard a noise . . . people talking! But her first emotion was one of terror, for she had heard many reports of hostile Indian tribes. She turned to escape back into the jungle but then, as she explained to Jean later, she reflected for a moment and decided that nothing worse could possibly happen to her than had already happened, that anything was better than continuing as she was. This is certainly a glimpse of the old Isabel, practical and strong-minded. She decided, she explained to Jean, that "alarm was childish," and went forward to the bank of the river where two Indians were launching their canoe after passing the night on the shore. They must have been amazed, and perhaps alarmed as well, seeing a strange apparition staggering out of the forest. A woman, skeleton-thin, in rags, her long matted hair hanging around her shoulders, supporting herself on a stick. A white woman!

The two Indians and their wives had left Canelos when the smallpox struck and were headed now for Andoas. They stood hesitating, not knowing what to do in this strange case. She begged them, in broken Quechua, for she was too exhausted to speak properly, to take her to Andoas. As Jean put it, "They received my wife on board with kindness truly affectionate, showed every attention to her wants, and conducted her to that village."

They must have taken immediate charge of her, for she was totally exhausted. She could not swallow the meat they offered, so they provided broth; they helped her to lie in the canoe on a bed of straw. The journey to Andoas took three or four days and Isabel was delirious much of that time. The women bent over her solicitously, offering her water to drink, covering her with garments of their own to keep off the river chill, fanning away the insects.

I often think of this testimony to human kindness. Was it perhaps partly due to Isabel's own sympathetic character that natives, so often described as hostile, treated her with such consideration? Whatever their reason, she ever after referred to them as "my dear Americans."

By the time the Indians reached the mission of Andoas and went ashore there, Isabel was far enough recovered to think about her future journey, which would still require many weeks of strenuous travel. She must have thought of her father waiting on the galliot in Loreto, expecting not his daughter only, but a whole troop of relatives and acquaintances from Riobamba. How to tell the general, who was now an old man, that he had lost two sons and a grandson, and that his daughter was the only survivor of the party for whom he had made such careful preparations? I hope he never realized that the whole tragedy was very probably brought on by his own passage through the town of Canelos when one of his Indian bearers left the germs of the small-pox behind.

In fact, General Grandmaison had already been alerted to the disaster. More than a month before Isabel reached Andoas, the doctor and Joaquin had been there. They had not been wrecked or perished, as Isabel imagined. The doctor, confirming her opinion of him, went on down the river and made no rescue effort. It was up to the faithful Joaquin to round up a canoe and oarsmen; then they must return against the current. By the time they arrived at the party's last shelter, there was no sign of anyone. However, Joaquin found it easy to trace them along the shore and into the forest, and here he came upon the group of corpses, now unrecognizable. He assumed that all had died, including Isabel. He returned to Andoas and the news went out to all the missions and to the general at Loreto, far down the river.

Isabel, when she reached Andoas with her Indian friends, planned to rest and recruit her strength before attempting further travel. She had looked forward to a friendly welcome at the mission, but she again had bad fortune. The mission-ary was the worst sort of representative of the church in the New World, remaining there only for his own profit. Isabel had evidently regained her strength of mind; she would not endure injustice, especially to her Indian rescuers. Jean describes the incident:

"Madame Godin, stripped of almost everything, not knowing otherwise how to testify her gratitude to the two Americans who had saved her life, took from her neck two chains of gold, such as are usually worn in this country, of about four ounces weight, and gave one to each of them, whose admiration at the richness of the present equalled that they would have experienced had the heavens opened before them; but the missionary in her very presence took possession of the chains, and gave the poor Americans in lieu about three or four yards of coarse cotton, such as is manufactured in the country, and called Tucuyo. Conduct thus infamous exasperated my wife to such a degree that she instantly demanded a canoe and men, and the next day set out for Laguna."

The next stop was many days' journey down the Bobonaza and then the Pastaza. At Laguna, where the Spanish head of missions had his headquarters, Isabel met very different treatment. She remained there six weeks, trying to live down her trials and the fever that persisted. Monsieur Romero, the chief of the mission, took the greatest care of her, sending word to her father at Loreto that his daughter, alone among the travelers, had miraculously survived.

Meanwhile, as she returned to health, she returned also to her preoccupation: to find and join her husband. As souvenirs of her days in the jungle, she kept the sandals she had fashioned and the cotton petticoat that an Indian woman at Andoas had made for her; she kept these for the rest of her life. Now, however, she wanted simply to get on with her journey.

Monsieur Romero, meanwhile, wrote to the general telling him that Isabel was out of danger and asking him to send someone to accompany her to the Portuguese galliot. However, on his own responsibility, he discussed with Madame Godin the course he felt she should pursue. He pointed out to her that, while he greatly admired her courage, she was still merely at the beginning of a long and tedious voyage; that, though she had already traveled almost four hundred leagues, she still had four or five times that distance to pass before she reached Cayenne. He reminded her that she had just escaped the perils of death and if she went on, there could be fresh dangers. Finally, he offered to have her escorted back to Riobamba in perfect security.

Isabel replied in positive terms, as might be expected. She was surprised at his proposals, she said. The Almighty had preserved her alone amid perils in which all her former companions had perished; the first of her wishes was to rejoin her husband and that was why she had begun her journey; and finally, she said, if she were to abandon her plan, she would consider herself guilty of counteracting the views of Providence, and render useless that help she had received from her two dear Americans and their wives, as well as all the kindness for which she was indebted to him.

Since Isabel had been at the mission for six weeks, Monsieur Romero was probably not surprised by this outburst, different as it may have been from the reactions of most eighteenth-century ladies. There was no use trying to persuade her. He gave up gracefully and ordered a canoe to be equipped to take Madame Godin, without stopping anywhere, to the Portuguese galliot at Loreto. He informed the Governor of Omaguas of her coming, and that she was proceeding without stops, and the Governor thereupon dispatched a canoe to meet her, loaded with refreshments. She reached Loreto, was reunited with her father, and the galliot finally set out down the Amazon after its years of waiting.

From here on Isabel's progress was comfortable, even luxurious, when one considers the thousands of miles of rough wilderness through which the galliot must pass. She did have to put up with one irritation: the French doctor was aboard. He had had the effrontery to turn up in Laguna while Isabel was recuperating there, bringing some of her property that he had taken down the Bobonaza when he and Joaquin left to get help. He brought, she recalled later, "four silver dishes, a silver saucepan, a velvet petticoat, one of Persiana, and one of taffety, some linen, and other trifles, belonging to her brothers as well as herself." He added that "all the rest were rotten, forgetting that bracelets, snuff-boxes, and rosaries of gold, and ear-rings set with emeralds, were not subject to rottenness." He had the further gall to ask her to take him down the Amazon with her on the galliot. Isabel later told Jean what she had said:

"Go your ways, Sir; it is impossible that I can ever forget that, to you, I owe all my misfortunes and all my losses; manage henceforward as you may, I am determined you shall make no part of my company."

After six weeks' association with Isabel Godin, Monsieur Romero knew of her soft streak. The doctor had become a friend of his. He argued with her at length and she, remembering how much she owed to him for his care of her, reluctantly agreed that the doctor should come along.

Nothing further is said about this and I find it fascinating to imagine how the three of them, the general, Isabel, and the rascally doctor, could have traveled together for months on a fairly small ship. Did they ignore one other, Isabel and her father staying on one side of the deck while the doctor stayed on the other? Did they eat meals together? We will never know, for the little notebook Isabel is said to have kept has vanished.

The journey down the river might be considered the original tourist excursion on the Amazon. Jean describes it: "I learn from her that . . . till she reached Oyapok, throughout a course of nearly a thousand leagues, she wanted for nothing to render her comfortable, not even the nicest delicacies, and such as could not be expected in the country; wine and liquors which she never uses, fish, game, etc. were supplied by two canoes which preceded the galliot. The Governor of Para, moreover, had sent orders to the chief part of the stages at which they had to halt, with additional refreshments."

Meantime, there must have been great excitement among the missionaries as word was handed along the Amazon that a white woman was approaching—a heroine, for she was already considered that—who had survived by a miracle after nine days alone in the immense jungle of the river basin. Rumors soon crossed the ocean to the continent. In London, Isabel's exploits—whatever they were, no one was certain—fascinated the members of London's coffeehouses. In Paris rumors went the rounds of the salons. "Peru"—a distant, mysterious country that few people had visited except the Spaniards who controlled the place. "The Amazon"—an almost mythical river where wild beasts and hostile Indians roamed. This white woman, Isabel Godin (a French name) crossed the whole jungle alone . . . had nothing to eat but coconuts . . . strangled a jaguar with her bare hands . . . swam a hundred kilometers down the great river pursued by crocodiles. . . .

La Condamine frequented Madame Geoffrin's fashionable

salon, where he heard such tales. He could set the gossips straight as to the Amazon, since he had explored it, and he of course knew Isabel. She could not have done these things, but what did she do? He eventually wrote to Jean asking for a full account of Isabel's adventures and that is why we have Jean's letter giving the facts.

There is no record of when Isabel, the general, and the doctor left Loreto on the galliot. It was probably sometime in April. It was about three months until they reached the end of their journey. Isabel, now fairly well recovered from her ordeal, must have enjoyed the river voyage. She had always been curious about the world and now she was seeing an extraordinary part of it. Now at last she could relax, allow herself to be coddled and cared for, walk the deck enjoying the warm tropical air, or make notes in her little notebook and perhaps sketch in the birds and animals she saw along the shore. She waved to the fishermen, native women washing clothes, and brown naked children swimming.

The galliot must have met many small craft and a few sizable passenger ships, though perhaps none the size of the Portuguese vessel. It may have been as much as sixty feet long, decked over, with a half-dozen tiny cabins. The two masts and sails were for working the boat upriver against the current. On this downriver voyage, the sails were not raised. Thirty oarsmen (this figure we know from Jean's description) paddled constantly and the galliot was also rapidly propelled by the current. The steersmen knew from experience when to follow the middle of the river, and when to hug the shore, which might be a mile or two away, to take advantage of the shifting currents. They were adroit and the passengers felt perfectly secure if somewhat bored by the monotonous weeks of travel. How different from Isabel's brief journeys in the canoe and on the raft after her ill-fated party left Canelos!

As the Amazon neared its mouth, the river grew wider and wider, turning into a bewildering series of lagoons, islands, peninsulas, deltas, straits, inlets. While the galliot was still a hundred miles upstream, the tide rushed upstream and receded, carrying with it sand and mud and dead vegetation far out into the Atlantic.

Now there were no more mission settlements along the shore. The animals, birds, and fish of the inland river gave way to ocean life. Screaming seagulls followed the galliot for scraps of food thrown overboard. Pelicans flew in parade formation along the river. Natives who paddled out to the galliot to sell fish were different from those upstream. They carried knives, wore European-style shirts, and spoke phrases of Portuguese.

Finally, the galliot swept around a curve in the river and entered the ocean, which must have been a moment of particular excitement for Isabel. Her first sight of an ocean and now she could again start to count the days until she and Jean would meet!

The original captain of the galliot had been replaced by a pilot specially versed in waters along the coast who would take command and sail the vessel the three hundred miles from the Amazon to Oyapok in French Guiana.

Jean goes on with the story:

"A little beyond the mouth of the river, at a spot off the coast where the currents are very violent, [the captain] lost one of his anchors, and as it would have been imprudent to venture with only one, he sent a boat to Oyapok, to seek assistance, which was immediately forwarded. Hearing by this means of the approach of Madame Godin, I left Oyapok on board the galliot belonging to me, in view of meeting her, and on the fourth day of my departure, fell in with her vessel opposite to Mayacare. On board this vessel, after twenty years' absence, and a long endurance on either side of alarms and misfortunes, I again met with a cherished wife, whom I had almost given over every hope of seeing again. . . . We anchored at Oyapok the 22nd July 1770."

SIXTEEN

JEAN AND ISABEL GODIN were finally reunited. Isabel left no written word except, perhaps, in the small notebook now lost to us. Jean, however, wrote to La Condamine: "In her embraces I forgot the loss of the fruits of our union, nay, I even congratulated myself on their premature death as it saved them from the dreadful fate which befell their uncles in the wood of Canelos beneath their mother's eyes, who certainly could never have survived the sight."

Isabel had been almost ten months traveling from Riobamba to Oyapok. France, where she had longed to be, was now only across the wide Atlantic Ocean. However, it was almost three years before Jean and Isabel finally left Guiana. Isabel's health, still precarious, did not allow her to take the long ocean voyage and Jean was engaged also, with legal difficulties. Finally, they departed for the continent on a vessel that made the voyage in six weeks, the usual time for a crossing. Jean must have done his best to spare Isabel the hardships of ocean travel and to prepare her to meet his family and friends. Her father, the general, accompanied them on the voyage, for "finding old age creep on apace," as Jean put it, he was of no mind to return to Riobamba.

On June 2, 1773, the couple arrived in France, at the port of La Rochelle. It was thirty-eight years since Jean Godin had left Saint-Amand Montrond, a young man of twenty-one, and set out on the frigate *Portefaix* to find adventure and to see the world.

Jean's family had forgotten him. After the long years he had become simply a name, a man who left home more than a generation ago. His mother, father, and two of his brothers had died. However, some property still belonged to him, and he and Isabel, along with her father, settled down in a house in the center of town. If Isabel ever saw Paris I do not know of it. Perhaps Saint-Amand, peaceful and quiet, was more to her taste at this time of life. Her father remained with them for some years, until he died. The younger brother of the nephew who had died in the jungle arrived in Saint-Amand and was put under her care. He was nine years old and she turned to him with all the frustrated love she had lost when her own children died. This boy, Jean Antoine, lived to grow up, married a local girl, and started the line of descent that has continued to this day.

Jean's fortunes were much depleted by the expense of caring for his father-in-law and his wife, and by the lawsuit he had had in Cayenne against the miserable Tristan, who not only did not deliver his letters to Isabel, but cheated him in business. Fortunately, through La Condamine's influence, he was granted by King Louis XV a pension of seven hundred francs a year, a generous sum, "in consideration of his work as a geographer with the French Geodesic Mission."

Jean and Isabel lived for twenty years in Saint-Amand. There is still discussion, two centuries later, of Isabel as she was then. Some townspeople remember word passed down by their forebears that the heroine of the Amazon regained her health and spirits. Others are convinced that she never recovered: she was a recluse, she was covered with scars from the bites of poisonous insects, she had a facial tic, which intensified when anything related to the jungle was mentioned. In any case, she endured no more dreadful experiences, but lived comfortably with Jean and her nephew.

In these last years of her life, she was surrounded by family, this time not Spanish but French. Her portrait hung in the salon at Saint-Amand Montrond, and a picture of her was incorporated in a stained glass window in the family's small château. The sandals she had worn in the jungle and the cotton petticoat made for her at Andoas were always prominently displayed.

Isabel and Jean both survived until old age. They died in 1792, within a few months of each other, Jean at seventy-nine, Isabel at sixty-four.

The past was not forgotten. In his will, made some years before his death, Jean left much property to Isabel, with the note: "Because of the good marriage there has always been between us, and because of her sufferings in her journey to come and find me in the isle of Cayenne . . . I am sorry that I cannot give her more."

While pondering my notes on the lives of the Expedition members, I carried on from Mexico an interesting correspondence with Monsieur Marc Lemaire, Isabel Godin's distant nephew. We exchanged details of our findings. We wrote, tentatively, about the possibility of meeting in Paris, but I had already taken my research trip to France. Our letters were easy and relaxed; I wrote in English, Monsieur Lemaire replied in French. I learned the following details from him.

From Isabel's nephew, Jean Antoine, came a line of collateral descendants who continued to live at Saint-Amand, all of them cherishing the story of "Aunt Godin." A grandnephew, Gilbert de Grandmaison, wrote, around 1830, a book called *An Unknown Drama: the Adventures of Madame Godin des Odonais née Isabel de Grandmaison*. Although he was the author of a number of other books, this one was never published. His son, Félix, Isabel's great-great-nephew, grew up hearing the story, not only of Isabel's journey, but of the Grandmaison family and life in Riobamba. He decided, at the romantic age of eighteen, to set out for South America to look up these long-lost relatives.

To make the trip, he signed on as a sailor—the story refers to him as "pilot" but he must have shipped as a common seaman. The ship was the *Océanie*, a three-masted bark, eight years old, equipped for a long voyage, sailing from Bordeaux. It was headed for San Francisco and the gold fields by way of Cape Horn, with stops at Valparaiso, Callao, Guayaquil, and Panama. Félix planned to disembark (or perhaps jump ship) at Guayaquil, and from there go up to Quito in what was by then the country of Ecuador, to drop in on his cousins.

The *Océanie* left Bordeaux on July 23, 1848, in order to arrive at the Horn in the month of October, after the spring equinoctial storms. The voyage was uneventful except for one accident. It was recorded in the log that on October 10, as the ship rounded the Cape, Félix de Grandmaison fell from the mast and disappeared, carried away by a giant wave. A letter written to him on August 6 by his sister and mother, addressed in care of Messieurs Thomas LaChambre, merchants at Lima via Panama, was returned to Saint-Amand marked "unclaimed." It was full of wise advice to a young man seeing the world, including messages to the newfound relatives and the reminder that the Grandmaison ancestors had been important, Don Pedro having been governor of the province of Guayaquil at the time of Isabel's marriage.

The loss of Félix at sea was a terrible blow to his family. They not only mourned the loss, but they became convinced that misfortune and tragedy would follow any attempt of the two branches of the family, at Saint-Amand and Riobamba, to get together. They recalled that Isabel's two brothers and one of her nephews had died in atrocious conditions in the Amazon forest while going from Riobamba to Europe; and now her great-great-nephew had perished off Cape Horn while journeying from Europe to Riobamba. No plan was ever made after that for the families to meet.

This might have ended the story of Isabel Godin, but it does not. In recent years she has inspired new interest, and a relationship has developed between Riobamba, Ecuador, and Saint-Amand Montrond, France. They have become sister cities, taking Isabel Godin as their "mascot," and founding a club to honor her, with the name "Amitié Berry-Chimborazo," which refers to friendship between the provinces in the two countries. Citizens of the French city have gone on tours to the Andean city, and visitors from Riobamba have been entertained in Saint-Amand. The Isabel Godin Cultural Center in Saint-Amand is matched by the Isabel Godin Technical Institute in Riobamba. At Monsieur Lemaire's suggestion, I joined the club (the first foreigner to do so) and began to receive their semiannual news booklet printed in French and Spanish devoted to information about Isabel Godin, Jean Godin, and the members of the French Geodesic Mission. It seemed a lively group, and I enjoyed correspondence with their president, Marcel Robin. I detected in myself an urge to go to France again. The occasion soon arose. In August 1992, the city of Saint-Amand Montrond would hold a full two weeks of commemorative events on the two-hundredth anniversary of the deaths of Jean and Isabel.

SEVENTEEN

Paris and Saint-Amand Montrond, August 1992

THE RUE DE BOURGOGNE was empty except for a small boy carrying a long loaf of bread nearly his size. A taxi sped by with a screech of brakes as it turned a corner. It was almost noon and I sat looking out the window in the lobby of the Hôtel du Palais-Bourbon waiting for Monsieur Marc Lemaire to pick me up and take me to his home in Marly-le-roi for lunch. I realized as I sat there that it was almost a year since I had last waited here, that time for a cab to take me to the airport terminal for my flight home to Mexico. Last August I had no thought of coming this way again, but here I was, on my way to Saint-Amand Montrond to attend the events that would take place there in observance of Jean and Isabel Godin's deaths two centuries ago. I was expected in Saint-Amand, a hotel room was reserved. Monsieur Robin, president of the club Amitié Berry-Chimborazo, would meet me at the station. Here in Paris, Monsieur Lemaire and his wife were waiting to entertain me.

While I sat at the window—it was still early, I was ahead

of time as usual—I tried to guess what Isabel's great-nephew would be like. I had few clues from our correspondence. He would not be a young man. Probably he was retired. Did he care about his distant ancestor or was the whole thing something of a bore? No doubt as he drove into the city to pick me up he was just as curious as I, wondering why an American woman living in Mexico would go out of her way to cross the ocean and visit a small French city, there to join in the observances of his great-aunt's death. I wondered why myself. Isabel's story had continued to become more engrossing as I went on with my quest. Perhaps this is true of all research into matters of history: imagination fleshes out the details until they become real, even though they do not entirely match the facts. This was the first time I had delved deeply into the life and character of a long-dead person. I felt that if Isabel and I had the chance to meet we would talk easily. I would have many questions to ask. Is there some communication possible through time? I leave such considerations aside; they are too arcane. I thought instead about the personal qualities a woman like Isabel must have had to make her an enduring heroine. Her exploits were remarkable, but other people have had harrowing experiences and miraculous escapes and only achieved temporary fame. Isabel Godin, who was not even French, has achieved permanent status as heroine of a small French city.

Was that Monsieur Lemaire coming up the steps? No, it was a young man speaking Italian, asking the way to the Rodin Museum.

"In the next block," Madame Duval at the desk told him, "just at the end of this street." She turned to me with interest. "You are waiting for someone?"

"Yes," I said, "but I'm not sure exactly who."

At that moment a man of about sixty-five, well dressed,

but with a look of uncertainty, came into the lobby and our eyes met. Monsieur Lemaire. He smiled, we shook hands. I knew right away that we would get along.

Marly-le-roi is a suburb about half an hour by car or train from the city. On the drive out there Monsieur Lemaire said many things in exceptionally rapid-fire French. I nodded and smiled and inserted a "Oui?" or "Vraiment?" here and there. I followed some though not all of his remarks, but assumed that the subject was Isabel until I caught the word "chien." A dog? That couldn't be Isabel. I quickly said that I was very fond of chiens. Turned out I was to meet Tutu, the old family pet. I hoped I would understand our discussions of Monsieur Lemaire's great-aunt better than this poor beginning.

At Marly-le-roi, in the Lemaires' apartment, I met Marc's wife, Sylviane (we had progressed to first names) and found her to be a sympathetic, motherly woman eager to revive her memories of the English language from forty years before, when she had spent some months in London. As we enjoyed an aperitif we progressed easily from initial formality to relaxed talk punctuated with laughter. There's nothing like two people speaking each other's language after decades without practice to bring out the lighter side.

While Marc was picking me up, Sylviane had been preparing a wonderful feast of many courses, melon balls, shrimp, roast beef, salad, cheese, apple tart, each item on the menu with its appropriate wine.

Time passed. It was getting late in the afternoon. Tutu was asleep under Marc's chair. We were all three feeling very friendly and the table was covered with half-empty bottles of wine. Over lunch I had learned that Marc Lemaire was not only interested in his ancestor—she was the object of his research. He went every day by train into Paris to delve into his family history in libraries and archives, going back to the time of Isabel and beyond. Who wouldn't enjoy looking up a family tree if it included such people as the archbishop of Guatemala, assorted nobility, and even a distant link with Louis XIV? I agreed to look up a few records in Mexico City to add to Marc's material and we made tentative plans for the Lemaires to come to my part of the world.

When Marc and Sylviane dropped me off at my hotel it was merely "á demain." The next day I was going to Saint-Amand for the Grand Opening and they were, too. We would therefore meet in Saint-Amand Montrond.

As I rode south on the train through the rolling hills of the château country, I thought again of the three years that had passed since I first saw Isabel's portrait in Cuenca and felt a rising interest in the French Mission. Here I was, as the result of that chance encounter, thousands of miles from home, going to see new friends in a city that I had not known existed.

Saint-Amand Montrond is a small city of twelve thousand, about two and a half hours by train southwest of Paris. It is in the exact center of France and has a monument to prove it. There are ruins of everything back to Roman times and Julius Caesar is said to have ascertained, through his scouts I guess, that this was the middle of Gaul. Perhaps the original draft of his statement said, "All Gaul is divided into three parts and Saint-Amand is in the middle." It is in beautiful country on the river Cher, formerly sheep country, and my club membership card shows a sheep and a llama dancing together. Now the sheep have given way to various small factories and many acres of sunflowers.

I was duly met at the station by Germaine Robin, wife of

our club president, and driven to a hotel facing on the town square. This part of Saint-Amand is modern, but the old city is only a few blocks away. I had already noticed a street named for Jean Godin, and Germaine showed me a small plaza presided over by a bust of Isabel. It was the work of a visiting sculptor from Ecuador, she told me.

In the late afternoon I attended the opening of the grand exposition in the "Centre Culturel Isabel Godin." The exhibit included pictures of Jean, Isabel, La Condamine, and the rest of the French scientists; a collection of books and articles about them; material from the town archives; and Indian weavings adorning the walls. The show was well attended. The mayor gave a speech and so did Marcel Robin. Wine and cookies were served and everyone spoke knowledgeably of the Expedition. It might have taken place last year, not a couple of centuries ago.

Later that evening the Lemaires and I went together to the spectacle that took place in the courtyard of the ancient town hall. It was called "Le Plus Long Amour" and followed the adventures of Jean and Isabel in a combination of dancing, music, oratory, acting, and slides projected on a big screen. It sounds strange, but it was very effective. There would be nine performances of this show during the next several days.

My new friends spent a week showing me the sights: a couple of châteaux, an abbey, the old fortress in the middle of town on top of the "mont rond" that gave the city its name.

In the evenings I went up to the old Market Square where no doubt Isabel did her shopping. There I sat in a sidewalk cafe and drank tea (the stomach can take just so much wine unless you are native French) and dreamed about the past and watched another spectacle. The one about Isabel was very professional and cost twelve dollars. This one was amateur and free. It featured young people dashing in from the side streets pretending to be square-rigged ships, and Columbus striding around with assorted adventurers. The musical background of flute and drums might have been from another era, two hundred years ago.

One day I mentioned that I would like to get into the house where Jean and Isabel lived during their twenty years in Saint-Amand. It is around the corner from the Cultural Center. A plaque on the gate reads "Isabel de Casa Mayor and Jean Godin des Odonais, member of La Condamine's expedition to the equator, finished their life of adventure here in 1792." A sign above it shows that the building is now the Jeanne D'Arc Primary School.

A group of us obtained permission to explore the house. Bernard Vannier, one of the club members, opened the gate with an old-fashioned key, and we entered a flagged court-yard.

"It was probably an orchard in Isabel's time," Bernard said. He and Marcel dragged the children's jungle gym aside so that I could take photos of the facade, then we entered the dwelling. A note over the door dated the house at 1671. It is now a decidedly modern kindergarten, with little brightly colored chairs and desks, and children's drawings pinned to the wall.

We climbed up a circular staircase with a curiously shaped wooden handrail. "Isabel used this," Bernard remarked. We had discovered no mementos on the ground floor, and the second floor offered no furniture of the eighteenth century, no collection of old tomes, no family portraits leaning against the wall, no odds and ends of antique chairs and dilapidated tables.

Well, at least it was the house. The rooms were unchanged. Isabel and Jean, the old general while he lived, and the new young nephew had all gone up and down these stairs.

We climbed the final steep flight of steps to the attic. "If there's anything of interest it will be here in the grenier," Marcel said, brushing a spider from his shoulder. "But probably everything is gone now . . . although here in Saint-Amand we do not throw the past away easily."

The attic was dusty, dimly lit by a couple of narrow dormer windows. Cobwebs hung in corners, and a few broken children's desks leaned against one wall. A large doll lay forgotten by the stairs.

Under the far window I noticed an old trunk hanging open. It was an outmoded shape, huge, heavy, with ponderous straps. It gave off a pungent smell of leather blended with mold. Looking inside I saw only cobwebs and a blank scrap of paper.

I imagined the trunk loaded on a diligence, after the long sea voyage, for its ride over the rough roads from the port of La Rochelle in the hot summer of 1773, to its final destination in the middle of France. It had been abandoned here in the attic, probably because it was too cumbersome to haul down the stairs and, besides, it wasn't needed, no one was going anywhere. All the long journeys were over.

Back home in Mexico after my excursion to Saint-Amand, I sorted my notes for the last time and came across something I had missed before, although I had had a copy of it made at the Academy. It summed up, I thought, the boundless ambitions of those eighteenth-century scientists. Paris in those days was infatuated with science. Many private citizens had their own more or less elementary physics laboratories and mineral collections. There were public meetings also, and I held in my hand an invitation put out by Monsieur L'Abbe de Lille in 1774, shortly after La Condamine's death, to a reception. At this meeting would be described "countries where nature, warmed by being nearer to the sun, provides more perfume to the fruit, more rich colors to birds, and even more activity to fish, a land of the most imposing beauties and the most terrifying horrors."

A wide range of subjects would be considered at the reception: "physical questions on the movement, weight, light, colors, sound, equilibrium of liquids, fire, air, water, meteors, magnets, optics, astronomy, plants, the human body, chemistry—all those subjects studied by Charles-Marie de La Condamine." The lecture would be given in the College of Louis the Great, and afterwards, concluded the notice, "Public Experiments will be made on these same subjects."

It must have been a lengthy meeting. I wish that I had been there.

Now I suppose my search for Isabel Godin is ended. There remain the unanswered questions that could so easily have been answered if we had met. But even without sitting down for a talk with Isabel or reading her lost journal I believe I have found her essential character. Isabel Godin was a survivor. She left behind an enduring legend of courage in atrocious circumstances. My reading and travels have been valuable, not only for the information gathered, but for the contacts with other people who find Isabel's story of lasting interest. I look forward to receiving the bulletin of the Amitié Berry-Chimborazo twice a year, and catching up on the latest contacts between Riobamba and Saint-Amand Montrond. Of course, I won't be going back to France again. This whole episode in my life is over . . . although perhaps when this book comes out I might deliver a few copies?

GLOSSARY OF FOREIGN WORDS

altiplano	high plateau
apachita	sacred spot on a mountain pass marked by a pile of stones
audiencia	Spanish colonial court or province
campanero bird	bird of the Andes whose call sounds like a bell
canicule	heat wave, dog days
cannonières	small tents used by some of the scientists
capybara	huge South American rat, largest living rodent
charqui	dried meat of llama, sheep, or pig
chasquis	Inca royal messengers
chicha	fermented corn drink
chirimoya	a tropical fruit, "custard apple"
cholo, chola	person of mixed Spanish-Indian race
chuño	freeze-dried potatoes
cinchona	tree from which quinine is made

cordillera	mountain range
cuy	guinea pig
espanto de la selva	jungle terror
galliot	shallow-draft ship for navigation on rivers and coastal waters
guasache	small animal resembling a rabbit
hornado	roasted whole pig
ichu	tough grass of the high country
Oriente	area to the east of the Andes; the low-lying eastern jungle surrounding the Amazon and its tributaries
paiche	huge river fish, also called pirarucu
piastre	silver coin of Spanish America
puchero	Peruvian stew
quart de cercle	quadrant, astronomical instrument
quechua	Inca language
ramada	shelter made of branches
soroche	altitude sickness
toise	measurement of length: 6.395 feet
verbasco	plant containing the chemical compound rotenone. Its juices were used to paralyze fish.
viruela	smallpox

BIBLIOGRAPHY

Alvara0do, Pio Jaramillo. *La Présidencia de Quito. Tomo I.* Quito: Editorial El Comercio, 1938.

André, Eugene. *A Naturalist in the Guianas.* New York: Scribners, 1904.

Apiano, Pedro. *La Cosmographie de Pedro Apiano.* Anvers: Aguila de Oro, 1575.

Aviles Mosquera, José M. *Maldonado y Palomino, Pedro Vicente, Datos Para su Cronologia y Principales Fuentes Bibliograficas.* Quito, 1987.

Bassières, L., Ancien Conservateur de la Bibliothèque Publique et du Musée de Cayenne. *Madame Godin des Odonais.* Imprimerie Cornouaillaise, Quimper, France: 1936.

Bennet, Wendell C., and Junius B. Bird, *Andean Cultural History.* New York: Natural History Press, 1964.

Bergnes, M. E. and L. C. *El Nuevo Viajero Universal en America.* Barcelona, 1833.

Bouguer, Pierre. *La Figure de la Terre.* Paris, 1749.

———. *Lettre a Monsieur . . . dans laquelle on discute divers points d'Astronomie Pratique.* Paris, 1754.

Brand, Lieut. Charles, RN. *Journal of a Voyage to Peru in the Winter of 1827*. Bath, England, 1985.

Carletti, Francesco. *My Voyage Around the World 1594–96*. New York: Pantheon, 1964.

Casa de la Cultura Ecuatoriana. *La Mision Géodésica Francesa*. Quito, Ecuador: Nueva Editorial, 1987.

Chevalier, August. *La Deuxième Centenaire de la Découverte du Caouchouc faite par Charles-Marie de La Condamine*. Paris: Révue de Botanique, 1936.

Cobban, Alfred. *The Eighteenth Century, Europe in the Age of Enlightenment*. New York: McGraw Hill, 1969.

Constable's *Miscellany of Original and Selected Publications in Various Departments of Literature, Science and the Arts*. Vol. XI. Edinburgh, 1827.

Cortambert, Richard. *Les Illustres Voyageuses*. Paris: E. Maillet, 1866.

Degrée du Meridien entre Paris et Amiens determiné par la Mesure de M. Picard et par les Observations de Mss. de Mauertuis, Durant, le Monnier, de l'Académie Royale des Sciences. Paris: G. Martin, Coignard et Guerin, 1740.

Denis, Ferdinand. *Voyages Imaginaires, Songes, Visions et Romans Cabalistiques*. Amsterdam, 1788.

Descola, Jean. *Daily Life in Colonial Peru*. New York: Macmillan, 1968.

Discours Prononcés dans l'Académie Francaise le xxi juillet MDCCLXXIV a la Réception de M. l'Abbé de Lille à Paris. Chez J. B. Brunet et Démonville, 1774.

Doublet, E. *Deux géodésiens Espanols*. Révue Scientifique no. 13, 14 juillet, 1934. Paris.

Eichler, Arturo. *Ecuador; a Land, a People, a Culture*. Quito: Libri Mundi, 1982.

Enock, C. Reginald. *The Andes and the Amazon, Life and Travel in Peru.* New York: Scribners, 1907.

Fernandez de Oviedo y Valdes, El Capitan Gonzalo. *La Historia Général y Natural de Indias Islas y Terra Firma del Mar Oceano.* Madrid: Imprenta de la Real Académia de la Historia, 1851.

Furneaux, Robin. *The Amazon.* New York: Putnam, 1970.

Garcia y Garcia, Elvira. *La Mujer Peruana a Traves de los Siglos.* Lima: Impr. Americana, 1924–5.

Godin, Jean. *Letter to the Duc de Choiseul,* signed but undated, in the National Archives, Paris.

Goodman, Edmond J. *The Explorers of South America.* New York: Macmillan, 1972.

Haskins, Caryl P. *The Amazon.* New York: Doubleday Doran, 1943.

Herndon, William Lewis. *Explorations of the Amazon.* New York: McGraw Hill, 1952.

Herring, Hubert. *A History of Latin America.* New York: Knopf, 1961.

Hingston, E. W. G. *A Naturalist in the Guiana Forest.* London, 1932.

Histoire de l'Amérique et du Château de Montrond. Saint-Amand (Cher), France: Imprimerie Destenay, Bussière Frères, 1895.

Humboldt, Alexander de, and Aimé Bonpland. *Personal Narrative of Travels to the Equinoctial Regions of the New Continent during the Years 1799–1804.* London, 1819.

Jesperson, James, and James Fitz-Randolph. *From Sundials to Atomic Clocks, understanding Time and Frequency.* New York: 1982. Originally published by Washington National Bureau of Standards, 1977. Monograph no. 155.

Jombert, C-A. *Antoine de Ulloa.* Paris, 1752.

Jos, Emiliano. *La Expédicion de Ursua al Dorado, la Rebélion de Lope de Aquirre,* Husca, Peru, 1927.

Juan, Don George, and Don Antonio de Ulloa. *A Voyage to South America.* London: Davis & Reyners, 1760.

Juan, Jorge. *Voyage Historique de l'Amérique méridional fait par ordre du roi d'Espaqne.* Paris, 1751.

Juan, Jorge, and Antonio Ulloa. *Noticias Secretas de América.* Madrid: Hijos de Minuesa, 1988.

Jussieu, A. L. de. *Notes sur la Vie de Joseph de Jussieu par Son Neveu, 1704–1779.* Paris: Archives of the Académie des Sciences.

Kendall, Henry M., Robert M. Glendenning, and Clifford H. MacFadden. *Introduction to Geography.* New York: Harcourt, Brace & World, 1962.

Labat, R., Père, de l'Ordre des Frères Pécheurs. *Voyage du Chevalier des Marchais en Guinée et Islas Voisines et à Cayenne fait en 1725, 26, 27.* Amsterdam, 1731.

La Condamine, Charles-Marie de. *Rélacion abrégée d'un voyage fait dans l'intérieur de l'Amérique méridionale.* Paris, 1745.

———. *Lettre sur l'émeute populair de Cuenca.* Paris, 1746.

———. *Mesure des trois premiers dégres du meridian.* Paris, 1751.

———. *Journal du voyage fait par ordre du roi a l'équateur.* Paris, 1751.

———. *Histoire des Pyramides de Quito.* Paris, 1751.

———. *Lettre a Monsieur M***.* Paris, 1774.

Laffant, Robert, ed. *The Illustrated History of Paris and the Parisians.* New York: Doubleday, 1958.

Le Magasin Pittoresque, tome XXII de Novembre 1854. *Adventures dé Mme Godin des Odonais née de Grandmaison.*

Lemaire, Marc. Text of lecture given December 1989 to the Académie des Sciences on the subject of his ancestor, Isabel Godin des Odonais. Paris: Archives of Académie des Sciences.

Leonard, Irving A., ed. *Colonial Travelers in Latin America.* New York: Knopf, 1972.

MacCreagh, G. *White Waters and Black.* New York, 1926.

MacEoin, Gary, and the Editors of Life. *Life World Library. Colombia and Venezuela and the Guianas.* New York: Time Inc., 1965.

Mathews, Edward D. *Up the Amazon and Madeira Rivers through Bolivia and Peru.* London: Sampson Low, Marston, Searle & Rivington Crown Publishers, 1879.

Maury, L.-F., Alfred. *Les Académies d'Autrefois - L'Ancienne Académie des Sciences.* Paris: Didier, 1864.

McBride, Barrie Sinclair. *History Today.* London: Bransen House, 1965.

Means, Philip A. *The Fall of the Inca Empire and the Spanish Rule in Peru, 1530–1780.* New York: 1932.

Medina, José Toribio. *The Discovery of the Amazon.* American Geographical Society Special Publication #17. New York, 1934.

Muller, Richard. *Isabel Godin.* Guayaquil, 1936.

Newman, James R. *The World of Mathematics.* New York: Simon and Schuster, 1956.

Ortega Ricaurte, Daniel. *La Hoya del Amazonas.* Bogota: Escuela Tipografica Salésiana, 1936.

Perrier, General G. *La Condamine et l'Expédition des Académicians français dans la Présidence de Quito (1735-1744)*. Paris: "La Révue Générale du Caouchouc" no. 125, Oct. 1936.

Pinkerton, John. *A General Collection of the Best and Most Interesting Voyages and Travels in All Parts of the World*. London: Longman, Hurst, Rees, Zorme and Brown, 1813.

Prudhomme, Louis Marie. *Voyage a la Guiana et a Cayenne*. Paris: 1798.

Shoumatoff, Alex. *The Rivers Amazon*. San Francisco: Sierra Club Books, 1978.

Skelton, R. A. *Explorers Maps*. London: Routlege & Kegan Paul, 1958.

Skinner, Joseph. *Present State of Peru*. London: Phillips, 1805.

Spruce, Richard. *Notes of a Botanist on the Amazon and Andes*. vol. II. London: Macmillan, 1908.

Thacker, John Boyd. *The Continent of America*. New York: William Evarts Benjamin, 1896.

Trystam, Florence. *L'Épopée du Méridien Terrestre. Le Proces des Étoiles*. Roman. Editions Seghers, Paris, 1979.

Ulloa, Antonio de. *A Voyage to South America*. London: Davis, 1772.

Verdoom, Frans, ed. *Plant and Plant Science in Latin America*. New York: The Ronald Press, 1945.

Von Hagen, Victor Wolfgang. *South America Called Them*. New York: Knopf, 1945.

Waugh, Evelyn. *92 Days, A Journey in Guiana and Brazil*. London, 1934.

Whymper, Edward. *Travels Amongst the Great Andes of the Equator*. Salt Lake City: Peregrine Smith books, 1987.

Wilson, Robert. *Voyages of Discoveries Round the World.* London: James Cundee, 1806.

Winsor, Justin. *The Amazon & Eldorado.* Boston & New York: 1884–89. (In his *Narrative and Critical History of America.*)

Zarate, Augustin de. *A History of the Discovery and Conquest of Peru.* London: Penguin, 1933.

Zuñiga, Neptali. *La Expédicion Cientifica de Francia del Siglo XVIII en la Présidencia de Quito.* Quito: Biblioteca Ecuador, 1977.

In addition, much unpublished, uncatalogued material, original letters, and reports, from the archives of the Académie des Sciences, Paris.

INDEX